IT TAKES
A CITY

IT TAKES A CITY

Getting Serious about Urban School Reform

Paul T. Hill
Christine Campbell
James Harvey

with
Paul Herdman, Janet Looney, Lawrence Pierce,
Carol Reed, and Abigail Winger

BROOKINGS INSTITUTION PRESS
Washington, D.C.

Copyright © 2000
THE BROOKINGS INSTITUTION
1775 Massachusetts Avenue, N.W., Washington, D.C. 20036
www.brookings.edu

Library of Congress Cataloging-in-Publication data

Hill, Paul Thomas, 1943–
    It takes a city / Paul T. Hill and others.
        p.   cm.
Includes bibliographical references and index.
    ISBN 0-8157-3639-8 (pbk. : alk. paper)
    1. Education, Urban—United States—Administration—Case studies.
    2. Education, Urban—Political aspects—United States—Case studies.
    3. Educational change—United States—Case studies. 4. Education and
state—United States—Case studies. I. Title.
    LC5131 .H48 1999   99-050587
    370′.9173′2—dc21   CIP

                      9 8 7 6 5 4 3 2 1

The paper used in this publication meets minimum requirements
of the American National Standard for Information Sciences—Per-
manence of Paper for Printed Library Materials: ANSI Z39.48-1984.

Typeset in Minion

Composition by Cynthia Stock
Silver Spring, Maryland

Printed by R. R. Donnelley and Sons
Harrisonburg, Virginia

Foreword

NEARLY FOUR YEARS AGO, Brookings made a long-term commitment to urban education. We set out to create options for city leaders—mayors, heads of cultural institutions, of philanthropies, and of businesses, and school board members and superintendents—who hoped to turn around failing big-city school systems.

We began our work at a time when lay takeovers of city public school systems were becoming common. School systems in Baltimore, Washington, Hartford, Cleveland, Boston, and Chicago had been taken over by groups of civic leaders appointed by mayors or state governments. This trend has continued, now including a second takeover of the Cleveland schools, a mayoral takeover in Detroit, and mayoral intervention in Los Angeles and Oakland. Other cities are likely to follow.

Lay takeovers of big city public education systems are measures of desperation. After decades of decline in school quality, citizens and public officials in many localities have concluded that something must be done to make sure that city children learn enough to function as adults in American society. But a takeover only replaces one set of decision-makers with another. It cannot improve education unless the people who take over have definite ideas about how to make more schools more effective. How can city leaders who are forced to take over school systems make a real difference? How, moreover, can educators and lay leaders in other cities turn troubled local education systems around before a takeover becomes a necessity?

This book, a sequel to *Fixing Urban Schools* (Brookings, 1998), is a practical guide for mayors, civic leaders, and school board members. The earlier book showed how "name brand" reform proposals, such as large-scale retraining of teachers, imposing standards, decentralizing, implementing new school designs, chartering, contracting out, and establishing vouchers, can all contribute something important to a reform strategy, but also showed that none of those proposals is likely to work all by itself. *Fixing Urban Schools* concluded that cities need hybrid strategies with three elements:

— strong performance incentives that reward adults for good school performance and force the closing and replacing of low-performing schools that cannot improve;

— major investments in the capacities of teachers and schools, including both the retraining of current teachers and principals and the recruitment of adults with superior education and diverse professional backgrounds; and

— school freedom of action that allows experimentation with new methods of teaching methods, staffing, and organization.

It Takes a City: Getting Serious about Urban Education Reform provides concrete examples of reform strategies that combined the strengths and avoided the weaknesses of the individual "name brand" proposals. Based on case studies of six reform initiatives—in Boston, Memphis, New York City District 2, San Antonio, San Francisco, and Seattle—it allows leaders elsewhere to learn from the experience of cities that have attempted fundamental education reform. It identifies the many good ideas tried by these cities and also shows how, regrettably, many initiatives based on those ideas were crippled or abandoned.

In addition, this book shows how city leaders can construct strategies strong enough to work and provides a menu of initiatives that create strong performance incentives, effective investments in capacity, and school freedom of action. It also shows how such initiatives can be combined to create powerful strategies that could truly transform urban education. Some of these strategies break the hermetic seal between the traditional public school system and the many other community assets that can contribute to children's education, including cultural institutions, colleges and universities, major businesses, and even independent school systems. Transcending the debate about privatization, these approaches treat all community assets as relevant to the education of children.

This book also applies lessons from the political and managerial failures of many citywide reform strategies. Only two years after the authors began to study the six cities, four of them have either abandoned or severely watered down their reform strategies. Based on the experience of these cities, and many others that have tried but failed to improve the performance of their public school systems, they draw a daunting conclusion: the normal politics of school systems cannot support fundamental reform. The book's final two chapters describe several independent institutions needed to support a city's reform strategy: a permanent communitywide reform oversight mechanism; a specialized data gathering and analysis organization; an incubator for new schools, a real estate trust to develop and maintain school buildings and lease them at fair prices to all publicly funded schools; and an inspectorate to make objective judgments about whether low-performing schools are capable of improvement.

In the coming year Brookings will develop more extensive concept papers for each of these institutions and show how they can be established and supported with a combination of public and philanthropic funds.

The authors are grateful to the many school district leaders, teachers, principals, and private citizens who provided information for our six case studies. Paul Herdman, Janet Looney, Lawrence Pierce, Carol Reed, and Abigail Winger prepared drafts of the studies. The authors would also like to acknowledge the contributions of reviewers Paul Schneider, Bruno Manno, David Bergholz, Adam Urbanski, Donald McAdams, and Frederick Hess, as well as the work undertaken by editor James Schneider, verifier Takako Tsuji, proofreader Carlotta Ribar, and indexer Bob Elwood for the Brookings Institution Press.

The project was supported by funds from the Alcoa Foundation, the Joyce Foundation, the Pew Charitable Trusts, and the Edna McConnell Clark Foundation.

The views expressed in this book are those of the authors and should not be ascribed to any of the persons acknowledged above or to the trustees, officers, or other staff members of the Brookings Institution.

MICHAEL H. ARMACOST
President

Washington, D.C.
December 1999

Contents

Preface

THIS VOLUME is the second in a trilogy designed to describe the politics of reform in urban school systems and clarify reform options
available to mayors and other community leaders who want to improve
school performance dramatically. A particular audience for the book
includes noneducators who find themselves unexpectedly in charge of
large urban school systems, the experience of former business and military leaders in recent years in Seattle and Washington, D.C.

Three years ago the Brookings Institution committed itself to working directly with city leaders responsible for reforming struggling school
systems. The trilogy, a by-product of that commitment, is intended to
follow this sequence:

—*Fixing Urban Schools,* published in 1998, defined the basic reform
options available to public schools and demonstrated how they were
supposed to work.[1] Written by Paul T. Hill and Mary Beth Celio, the
book aimed to defuse controversies about potentially valuable reform
features (family choice and school competition, for example) by demonstrating that, far from being inherently dangerous, their possibilities
depend on how they are practiced. The main features of *Fixing Urban*

Schools will be described more fully in the body of this volume; all that the reader needs to understand now is that the first volume made it possible for community leaders to consider perfectly acceptable choices normally thought to be beyond the pale because of the professional norms dominating the reform discussion and the politics of urban schools.

—*It Takes a City* develops lessons from the reform experiences in six American cities that have made concerted attempts to improve their public schools: Boston, Memphis, New York City District 2, San Antonio, San Francisco, and Seattle. Together these communities represent most of the major regions of the United States. They have also employed a variety of reform strategies, and their experiences should be instructive to leaders contemplating reform initiatives in other cities. *It Takes a City* analyzes strengths and weaknesses in urban reform strategies, suggests how other city leaders might create programs combining the most promising reform elements, and provides specific guidance to local leaders about how to design, carry out, monitor, and assess reform initiatives.

—The third book in the trilogy will be designed to show how city leaders can make sure reform initiatives are consistently pursued and improved rather than abandoned when they hit snags. The volume will suggest how communities can build new mixed public-private institutions to track the progress of reform; manage human resources, including teacher and principal recruitment and training; incubate new schools to replace failed ones; and provide access to needed facilities for all schools, including new ones. Due late in 2000, the book will also demonstrate how combinations of philanthropy and public support can maintain school reform as a front-burner issue.

Because every community is different, none of these books attempts to prescribe a single reform strategy. But the trilogy will identify elements that any successful strategy must have and challenges that every reform must address and overcome.

Plan of This Book

This book contains seven major chapters. Following this preface, the introduction defines the problem, asks what is wrong with urban schools, and insists that a school reform strategy is essential, even if educational improvement alone cannot dramatically alter the conditions for children and families in inner-city communities.

Chapter 1 defines the realities of reform in the urban school context, argues that Band-Aids and aspirins are being prescribed for life-threatening educational illnesses, and shows why most school reform proposals are not able to produce the outcomes they seek and thus lead to a constant search for new ideas.[2] It concludes with a description of several competing reform ideas, each of which claims to hold the key to urban school improvement.

Chapter 2 introduces the experiences on which this book is based: it describes the recent reform histories of the six cities studied by a team from the Center on Reinventing Public Education at the University of Washington's Daniel J. Evans Graduate School of Public Affairs. (The appendix provides more detailed reports on the six sites.) It concludes by formulating the lessons that can be drawn from frontline experience in these urban areas.

Chapter 3 moves beyond simple description to analyze the thinking behind the reform strategies in each of the six cities. It provides a comparative analysis of experiences in the communities, supplemented by the lessons learned during a series of decisionmaking simulations conducted with city leaders by Center staff. It also identifies the theories of action by which reform planners in each of the cities hoped to initiate events leading to school improvement. In doing so it illuminates reform possibilities by looking across the different efforts to identify ways in which strategic elements might be employed in new combinations to avoid what was described in *Fixing Urban Schools* as "zones of wishful thinking."

Zones of wishful thinking exist in every major education reform proposal. These are the areas in which reformers, eagerly anticipating the benefits of a particular proposal, assume complementary changes in individuals and society that cannot be guaranteed. Class-size reduction proponents, for example, assume that schools will reorganize instruction to take advantage of smaller classes or that teachers will somehow teach in different and more successful ways. Chapter 3 is an effort to think explicitly about how different reforms can be combined to anticipate and eliminate zones of wishful thinking by providing a menu of reform strategies from which cities can choose.

Chapter 4 attempts to move beyond wishful thinking and the realities of urban school reform by outlining and analyzing three new strategies that deserve serious consideration by civic leaders if urban school reform is to succeed.

The succeeding chapters attempt to demonstrate how these reform strategies can be chosen, carried out, sustained, and made to work. Chapter 5 argues that new community- and leadership-based groups need to be put in place to achieve reform. It shows how public, nonprofit, philanthropic, and for-profit resources can be combined to manage and sustain the most promising reform strategies presented in the preceding chapter.

Chapter 6 takes up the local politics of reform, starting with the problem of how to put ambitious plans into effect and sustain them long enough to make a difference. It insists that lasting long enough to hold an awards ceremony is not the mark of successful implementation. Successful reforms are those able to show an effect on school quality and student learning. This chapter begins by identifying the many political and managerial factors that have destroyed the effectiveness of local reform initiatives (including the reforms described in our six cities), and it ends by suggesting a communitywide strategy for sustained reform leadership and political support.

Chapter 7 then examines how community leaders starting at ground zero can take the first steps toward putting the ideas in this volume into effect. In addition, it shows how to get help designing and operating an effective reform strategy and describes Brookings' on-going effort, in collaboration with institutions such as the Education Commission of the States and the Council on Aid to Education, to provide ideas and help to communities.

Sources

This volume draws on three major sources. The principal source is the set of case studies completed by the authors on behalf of the Brookings

Institution. Initiated in 1997 and completed in 1998, the studies focused on the six cities, each of which was pursuing a nationally recognized, innovative, citywide reform strategy when the studies were launched. In each of these communities a new superintendent or civic coalition was leading a reform intended to create pressures, incentives, and investments to encourage individual schools to reform.

The case studies followed developments in each city for two years, through intensive interviews with educational, civic, and business leaders and associated literature reviews. For each study, staff from the Center on Reinventing Public Education analyzed each city's reform strategy, its history and current status, the extent to which it had affected teachers and students, and challenges to the reform's continuation. The body of this volume describes developments in each of the six cities in broad terms; the appendix presents detailed case write-ups.

This primary data source was supplemented by two others. The authors also drew on cases completed for an earlier study of decentralization initiatives in five other cities: Charlotte, N.C., Chicago, Cincinnati, Denver, and Seattle. Those studies were done in 1994 and 1995 by teams from the University of Chicago and the University of Washington on behalf of the Annie E. Casey Foundation.[3] Finally, we took advantage of seven simulation sessions of communitywide decisionmaking involving thirty-eight people in Denver, San Francisco, and Seattle. In these simulations, conducted between September 1997 and July 1998 by the Center staff, groups of senior educators, public officials, and community organization leaders worked through hypothetical but realistic local school scenarios requiring creation of new reform strategies.

Seattle is the only community studied in each source. San Francisco participated in the first and the third (implementation case studies and simulations), and Denver can be found in the second (decentralization) and third.

What we conclude after analyzing these three sources of data is sobering indeed. Cities are unlikely to get the results they need by relying on the main strategies now at their disposal. We cannot get there from here with today's discrete approaches. It is time to get serious about urban school reform.

Introduction

WHAT IS WRONG with the schools in urban America? Why do their problems appear so intractable? How is it that, after years of effort and expenditures of billions of dollars, we have so little to show for our efforts? Is anyone to blame for this lack of progress despite decades of reform? If so, who?

Troubling questions such as these have framed the debate about urban schools since at least the 1960s, when the existence of widespread poverty amidst wealth and plenty first began to be acknowledged in the middle-class culture that came to define the United States after World War II.[1] Fueled by hopes of eliminating poverty by attacking ignorance, people came to view education as a sort of Archimedean lever that could be applied against the forces of racism, reaction, and the status quo to create a society free of illiteracy—free, indeed, of want and hunger.

Disappointed Hopes

Although the ascension of the commitment to education could be seen most clearly in the Democratic Party's rapid progression from John

1

F. Kennedy's citation of the biblical injunction that the "poor are always with you" to Lyndon B. Johnson's declaration of a War on Poverty, the commitment flowered with equal passion in the Republican Party. If it was the party of Johnson that created the Elementary and Secondary Education Act of 1965 (ESEA), the Office of Economic Opportunity, and the Jobs Corps, it was the party of Richard Nixon that urged enactment of desegregation assistance in 1972, set out to guarantee a base for college students' financial aid, and established community grants for job training. And if Warren Magnuson of Washington and Edward Kennedy of Massachusetts served as archetypes of staunch Senate Democrats supporting Title I of ESEA, which has provided billions of dollars over the years to educate low-income urban and rural students, their matches were readily found on the Republican aisles in such stalwarts as Jacob Javits of New York and Richard Schweiker of Pennsylvania. Commitment to education as the nation's weapon of choice in the battle for equal opportunity respected and respects no partisan boundaries.

And yet more than three decades after the legislative triumphs that translated these ideals into national and state policy, the results fall short of what their sponsors had expected. Although it is true that urban schools face greater challenges in terms of the poverty of their students than they did in 1965, it is also true that the questions that gave rise to these education programs continue to be raised. Now they take on an even greater intensity. For today the stakes are higher, the poverty these programs were intended to attack has intensified, and the students involved are even more at risk. "What is wrong with urban schools?" remains our question. Why can't we fix them?

More Disturbing Questions

Today, for the first time, even more unsettling questions begin to insinuate themselves into the public consciousness. Does our schools' inability to teach poor students stem from problems in the system itself? Or is the problem deeper: society's inability to support the community structures that make effective schooling possible?

A disturbing question, and behind it an even more disquieting issue, rarely raised in polite company because its implications are so potentially ugly and contentious. Is the difficulty inherent in urban schools or in the students who attend them? Snap judgments about the second question are offered up every day in homes, restaurants, bars, country clubs, and community centers all over the United States; but it is almost never acknowledged as a serious question by either educators or analysts, perhaps because in the deep recesses of their minds we are afraid of the answer, unprepared to confront our own preconceptions about students who are different from ourselves—poor, or minority, and for the most part both.

Importance of Schooling for Disadvantaged Americans

This volume is about big-city schools in which low-income children and children of color make up the overwhelming majority of enrolled students. (The majority of African American students, but about one in five white students, are educated in central city schools.)[2] But similar dynamics can readily be seen in low-income rural areas, in which enrollment consists largely of low-income whites. What both urban and low-income rural areas share is an enrollment base challenged by cultural issues of class and income. In big-city schools these difficulties are magnified several times over by the massive racial insult of centuries of prejudice.

All young people need high-quality schools to develop to their full potential. Parents in well-to-do areas understand this intuitively, willingly bearing heavy burdens to make sure their children receive the advantages of the best education they can provide. Thus children of affluence benefit not only from the superior learning opportunities they receive in the home, during recreational activities, and on family vacations, but also from their parents' financial support, either in supporting first-class local public schools or paying tuition at independent, private, or parochial schools.

It is precisely because they do not get the out-of-school experiences middle- and upper-middle-income children receive that low-income students rely so heavily on the public schools. Formal learning opportunities for low-income minority young people are largely restricted to what they have the opportunity to learn in school, unsupplemented by museum trips, access to computers and the Internet at home, vacation visits to the nation's great landmarks and national parks, or opportunities to spend a few weeks traveling abroad.

And the evidence is by now abundant that urban students are not learning what they need to know—and that student learning and achievement are not improving in response to the reform efforts that have been mounted. It is time to get serious about what these challenges mean.

The Limits of Any School-Based Strategy

Many community leaders also know they must get serious about other factors that affect students' learning—poverty, limited English skills, immigrant status, illness or disability, unstable homes, transiency within neighborhoods and among members of the extended family, periods of migrancy, and the emotional turmoil invariably accompanying many of these problems. It is clear that since ESEA was enacted more than thirty years ago, the incidence of child poverty, single parenthood, and child abuse and neglect has increased, while basic services for children and families in poverty have not matched the growing need and may even have been neglected. Though these factors do not prevent learning, they almost invariably make it more difficult.[3]

There is a very real problem here. Urban schools educate disadvantaged students amidst very difficult circumstances. Defenders of urban schools and the educators there point out the challenges attendant on the poverty with which they have to contend. "How much can we realistically expect from urban schools, and how fast?" is frequently the formulation. But the question is asked in many different ways. "Is it reasonable to expect urban students to fare as well as their counterparts in more affluent circumstances?" "What about three decades of research demonstrating the importance of parent income and education to student learning?" "How can you ignore the recent evidence indicating that the mother's education is significantly correlated with student performance?"

These questions help explain the timidity of much conventional reform thinking. The hard fact is that many educators and policymakers simply do not expect inner-city students to be capable of learning very much. These young people, therefore, are caught in a classic double bind: the problems of their communities affect both the quality of schools and young people's ability to benefit from schooling. The larger economic system constrains the future of their communities and their communities' capacity to support decent schools.

In the face of these massive challenges, this volume insists that it takes a city to educate a child. This conclusion is grounded in three basic principles. First, we hold that school improvement is worthwhile in itself, indispensable to children, youth, and families, and an essential component of any urban improvement strategy. We find it impossible to conceive of any urban revitalization program that would not include within it a powerful school component.

Second, we caution that youth development and antipoverty strategies are as difficult to formulate and carry out as strategies for school improvement. Distinguishing plausible-sounding from potentially effective strategies in those areas requires serious cause-and-effect analysis, similar to what Brookings has done for urban education. As in education, it is not enough just to say that children and families need services. It is essential to know which services address what problems, how they are supposed to work, at what cost, and for whom.

Third, we do not believe that city leaders can focus on school improvement to the exclusion of all other matters, even if their intent is directed at improving student achievement. Schools cannot be let off the hook for not improving their own performance; city leaders must hold them accountable. But city leaders might also want to embed a school improvement strategy in a more comprehensive package of strategies that sets out to broker preschool, school readiness, and health and social services to ensure that public and private resources are directed to where they are most needed. A successful strategy addressing these problems will undoubtedly have more dramatic effects on student learning than a school improvement strategy alone. One of the three major options presented in this volume describes precisely such an approach.

Community leaders confident of how school reform strategies should fit together with youth and antipoverty initiatives should surely pursue broader agendas than education-based strategies alone. However, their starting point must be the schools. Indeed, the truth is, urban school performance is so miserable that no one would be justified in encouraging delay in addressing problems of school quality until the solutions to all other youth and family needs were in hand. Student achievement needs are simply too compelling to be ignored while awaiting a single best solution for every community problem.

The Realities of
Urban School Reform   1

DIANA LAM arrived in San Antonio in 1994 with a national reputation as a rising star in the school administration firmament. It was a
reputation launched at the Harvard Graduate School of Education where
she completed her training, followed by leadership posts in Massachusetts's Chelsea District and Dubuque, Iowa, and rounded out with
involvement with a variety of well-regarded reform organizations such
as the New American Schools Development Corporation. An immigrant
of Peruvian background, Lam appeared to be the perfect candidate to
head up the troubled San Antonio district, with its 60,700 students and a
twenty-year legacy of depressingly poor student-achievement results.

When she arrived, she reports, she found forty-five out of the ninety-
five schools in her district to be on the state's "watch list," so seriously
behind in student-achievement results that the state was considering
moving in to take them over. By 1998, following implementation of an
impressive standards-based effort conceived and led by Lam to raise student performance, only three of the schools were still under the state's
watchful eye. Despite this progress, just twelve months later, Lam's contract was bought out by a school board unaccountably dissatisfied with
her performance.

In New York City a similar scenario played itself out in the 1990s around school chancellor Ramon Cortines.[1] Like Lam, Cortines was nationally respected from his years in school leadership, in his case in San Francisco, where he rose through the system to become school superintendent. A member of the educational advisory board of New American Schools, Cortines was recruited to New York City by Mayor David Dinkins, and his contract continued when federal district attorney Rudolph Giuliani succeeded Dinkins. But following months of increasingly public wrangles between the chancellor and Giuliani about who was in charge of policy directions for New York's schools (and how much money should be spent on them), the mayor forced Cortines from his position.

Meanwhile, in New York City's District 2, a variation on the theme of leadership turnover was occurring. Anthony Alvarado, the highly successful superintendent of the district, moved on his own volition to San Diego to assume the newly created position of chancellor of instruction. He left behind some noteworthy successes in District 2, a small elementary and middle school district that he had turned around. The district's schools boasted the second-highest mathematics and reading scores in the city when Alvarado left. But questions remain about whether his reforms can survive the leadership transition. And can the achievement improvements he coaxed out of the system at the elementary and middle school levels be extended to high schools? American secondary schools in general—urban, suburban, and rural—are virtually uncharted reform territory, a great Dismal Swamp into which many a brave elementary and middle school reformer has ventured never to be seen or heard from again.

Years earlier, John Murphy had been recruited by a board of community and business leaders to lead a new reform initiative in Charlotte, North Carolina. He convened an advisory panel of national experts and at their advice created an ambitious new performance-based management system for the district. Under the plan, using combinations of public funds and private contributions, he brought new ideas, methods, and people to Charlotte. However, Murphy's abrasive personal style generated conflict within the school system, and groups of school employees led an effort to defeat pro-Murphy school board members. Murphy resigned, and though Charlotte community leaders remain determined to improve the schools, much of what they started had to be abandoned.

Leadership turnover and abandonment of reform initiatives are endemic in urban school systems. The average tenure of an urban superintendent is under five years. The stories of San Antonio, New York City, and Charlotte are not at all unusual. Few bold reform initiatives can survive the fire they ignite in the schools and the community. Only the reasons for the turbulence and abandonment change.

Milwaukee's former superintendent Howard Fuller was pushed out by teacher opposition to his reforms. He is convinced the teachers' union ran board candidates against him simply because of his insistence that the schools and professional educators were responsible for the poor performance of African-American children in their classes. "They take credit for the successes; they just can't turn their backs on the failures," said Fuller, a social worker who had never worked in a school system until he was tapped for the top school job in Milwaukee.

In 1996 a congressionally mandated reform board in the District of Columbia agreed on the need for strong leadership and recruited retired army general Julius Becton to straighten out the school system's Byzantine finances, teacher recruitment, and expenditure controls. However, Becton walked away from the school system in anger in 1998, fed up with the realities of administering public schools in the nation's capital. Bureaucratic incompetence within the school system (or hostility to his reform agenda) delayed the opening of schools three weeks at the beginning of Becton's second school year (the third time in five years the schools had not opened on time under Becton and his predecessor Franklin Smith). And Becton refused to accept what he considered to be attacks on his integrity in a city so poorly administered that its schools and the city itself had wound up, at the insistence of Congress, just short of supervision by bankruptcy judges.

No one can be certain whether the initiatives we have sketched would have dramatically improved school performance or whether the leaders associated with them would have remained effective. But one can be fairly certain that an institution or community that engages in serial abandonment of initiatives and regular rejection of leaders will not progress far.

Like a misconceived version of *High Noon*, the script and story lines rarely vary. The town is under siege. City leaders search for an idea or a person to turn the situation around. Enter Marshal Gary Cooper to the relief of the townspeople. But when Cooper needs their help, they turn their backs, go home, and close the doors, leaving him alone to face the bad guys arriving on the noon train. "Surely you'll help me," comments Cooper, ever a believer in the perfectibility of human nature, to the city fathers. "That's why we hired you," is the response. Tension in the town is nearly unbearable as the train arrives. But to the relief of everyone, Cooper carries the day. The surprise ending in the misdirected educational parallel of *High Noon* is that, despite success, the sheriff is forced to leave town because the people do not care for all that noise.

Why Public Schools Matter

The facts are overwhelming and hard to ignore. Low-income African-American, Hispanic, and non-Hispanic immigrant children make up the overwhelming majority of students in New York, Chicago, St. Louis, Cleveland, Detroit, Philadelphia, Houston, Dallas, New Orleans, Miami, Denver, Milwaukee, Los Angeles, and Atlanta. These students are half as likely as upper-income students to score at the basic skill level on the National Assessment of Educational Progress. After grade three, urban minority children are only slightly behind national averages, but they fall farther behind the longer they remain in school.[2]

—By age 17 the average test scores for minority students are no higher than average scores for white 13-year-olds.

—Only half the children who enter big-city high schools stay through graduation four years later.

—Minority students educated in city public schools are less than half as likely as other children from low-income groups to enter four-year colleges.[3]

Although some individual schools and neighborhoods have fought successfully against these trends, we are unable to identify any city that has made significant, sustained progress citywide.

The circumstances of public education in big cities are extremely challenging. In the largest cities over 30 percent of all children live in poverty, compared to less than 20 percent elsewhere.[4] Teacher salaries are seldom as high as in wealthier suburbs, so city schools often lose their best teachers. As a result, schools in the lowest-income neighborhoods are often staffed by shifting casts of new and provisionally certified teachers. City children are more likely than children elsewhere to have teachers who lack field-specific training, and the discrepancies are greatest in the most challenging fields, mathematics and science.[5]

The difficult circumstances of urban public education might provide a statistical "explanation" because poverty and minority status are correlated with poor performance. But correlation need not be causation: some minority and poor students succeed, and some schools succeed nearly as well with disadvantaged students as they do with richer, majority students. Further, this statistical explanation is not a justification for poor performance. Mothers and fathers are correct to worry about schools that do not teach their children. They have every right to be angry. Business and community leaders are also right to worry and be angry about a public education system that does not prepare children to become full participants in the social, economic, and political lives of their cities.

Although it is tempting to try to fix blame for this situation, the temptation needs to be rejected. Fixing blame does no good. Teachers, principals, superintendents, and school board members are operating within the inherited constraints of the system in which they have to work. Moreover, although it is easy for community critics to convince themselves that bad faith on the part of the educational establishment explains all of the schools' ills, a moment's reflection dispels that illusion. Who is more likely to have the greater commitment to children and learning: people who chose to enter teaching, or those who decided to make their mark in business, politics, government, or the armed services? The question answers itself.

The Many Approaches to Managing School Improvement

Hoping big-city public education systems will fix themselves is also an illusion. In fact, they might be constitutionally and politically incapable of doing so. It is clear that their problems cannot be expected to go away any time soon.

Some communities, such as Washington, D.C., and Seattle, have hired former military leaders to act as superintendents. Others, including Minneapolis and Hartford, Connecticut, have hired private firms to act in their place. Still others, with Chicago and Cleveland among the most notable, have eliminated elected school boards in favor of appointed boards.

There are many ways to try to manage the pain of promoting school reform, and local leaders have often rearranged leadership positions and shuffled staff—convinced, apparently, that the fundamental problem is leadership, not the very structure of the education system itself. If the problem lies with who is in charge, changing the leadership offers promise of improvement; but if the problem lies elsewhere, replacing superintendents, creating school-site councils, and pretending that generals, private firms, and appointed boards will do what educators, the public sector, and elected boards could not is simply an exercise in postponing the inevitable reckoning.

Apparently taking account of this, some reforms look more closely at the system. Communities have experimented with changing the relationship between individual schools and the school district's central administrative office. In an effort to wring more improvement out of schools, in the early 1990s Chicago created elected school-site councils and gave them control over significant amounts of money. Disappointed with the results, Mayor Richard M. Daley Jr. next replaced the elected board with an appointed board and put a chief executive officer in charge of advancing reform. Seattle is the most prominent of several districts that have arranged for money to follow students to the schools they attend.

Communities have also tried intervening directly in the processes of teaching and learning. Columbus, Ohio, and Miami, for example, have adopted the principles of "effective schools" research, which helps school staffs clarify goals and focus on instruction.[6] The Philadelphia schools and those in Edmonds, Washington, went through exhaustive communitywide processes to create new standards for student learning. Teaching has received a lot of attention. Los Angeles and Miami created financial incentives to attract teachers with specific skills. Not to be outdone, Philadelphia, Chicago, San Francisco, and Houston used parts of a $500 million Annenberg Challenge grant to create new opportunities for teacher learning.

All of these strategies have stimulated a great deal of activity, and some might ultimately lead to improved schools. But none seems remotely likely to lead to major across-the-board improvements in student performance because each leaves intact the fundamental assumption at the

base of public education in the United States: "What we have in our public school system is pretty good. As reformers, our task is to improve on
it a little here, tweak it a little there, and cajole a few small changes from
the system somewhere else—and everything will be just fine."

In fact, it is this assumption that accounts for the disappointing results of two decades of efforts to improve American schools. The institutional reality is that within the system—and often outside it too, for those
leaders coopted by the internal frame of reference—very few stakeholders are convinced of the need for profound alterations in the way the
business of education is conducted. They speak of the need for change,
but it is in the hope that someone else will change. They speak of "aligning" the system, but the system is not a mechanism of some kind that
needs only effective tuning to perform more efficiently. It is made up of
millions of students, teachers, and administrators, with all of their
strengths and weaknesses. And the stakeholders speak of greater unifor-
mity and standardization of policy and practice, all the while ignoring
new developments in organizational theory. Standardization and organizational Taylorism have given way to concepts of organizational complexity and the need to accommodate it. In this environment the reforms
that are possible are modest and incremental, modifications at the mar-
gin offering little promise of substantial improvement.

How else is one to explain the catastrophic performance of the schools
in the nation's biggest cities? Year after year, dropout rates are high, facilities are often dangerous and almost always unpleasant, and student
achievement is weak. In the face of these educational illnesses, which are
life-threatening for some students immediately and in the long term
stunting life's possibilities for most, the reforms bruited about at press
conferences and policy enclaves amount to little more than palliatives.

In a comparable emergency involving, for instance, public health the
reaction would be immeasurably more dramatic. Public leaders would
insist that the medical community mobilize armies of surgeons, cardi-
ologists, specialists in infectious disease, internists, and volunteers of all
kinds. The fact that leaders outside the health community seized the initiative would be applauded. Nobody would think twice about the cost
involved in this mobilization of resources. The insistence on specialists
and the involvement of community volunteers would be taken for

granted. Everyone would understand that extreme responses are required in the face of threats to the community's health and well-being.

But in the face of the disaster facing public urban education, our society acts as though a modified version of business as usual will be sufficient. Although an entire generation of students has started school and left since *A Nation at Risk* first raised the alarm, the educational community and the rest of society have satisfied themselves with tinkering at the margins. Discussion of reform is dominated by educational insiders. Costs have increased, but new funds have been funneled into familiar channels. We act as though a cure for our educational malaise can be found with a warm bath—with a promise to revisit the situation tomorrow if today's placebo does not do the trick.

Spinning Wheels, Churning Policy, and Relentless Circularity

None of these efforts has perceptibly narrowed the performance gap between inner-city public school students and other American children, or is likely to do so. In part this is because, as Frederick Hess has shown, city public education systems are caught in "policy churn":

> District policymakers constantly embrace politically attractive changes, producing prodigious amounts of reform at a pace inimical to effective implementation. . . .
>
> [Districts] recycle initiatives, constantly modify previous initiatives, and adopt innovative reform A to replace practice B even as another district is adopting B as an innovative reform to replace practice A. . . .
>
> Urban districts appear to do a number of things in a stop-and-start, chaotic fashion that is not part of any clear strategy to improve specific elements of school performance.[7]

Hess paints a disturbing picture of city superintendents and other education leaders working frantically to improve schooling but not achieving any leverage on the problem. Incapable of finding a purchase, they are caught, he concludes, in a "pattern of symbolic activity."

> Reform efforts are not the solutions to problems in urban schooling and are only incidentally about improving education at all. . . . The frenetic

embrace of new approaches is not productive, largely because the very institutional incentives that drive reform activity also make likely the failure of individual reforms. Policymakers are driven by professional and community pressures to initiate a great deal of activity, because it demonstrates leadership and steers the local education agenda onto professionally and politically comfortable ground.[8]

Many political and business leaders, both in urban areas and state capitals, have come to agree. As a result, actions by state legislatures and courts and by mayors' summits have led city governments to disband and take over school systems in Baltimore, Boston, Cleveland, Hartford, and other cities. Congress ordered a takeover of the District of Columbia public schools. "Academic bankruptcy" legislation recently enacted in Pennsylvania, New Jersey, and Maryland—and pending elsewhere—opens up the possibility of future takeovers.

Takeovers and the creation of new governing structures for public education are responses to policy churn, but they are no guarantee that it will end. New people will not necessarily have better ideas or be able to pursue bolder or more consistent strategies. The failures of takeover efforts in the District of Columbia, and the fact that the state of Ohio had to take over the Cleveland schools twice before it could find stable leadership, demonstrate the point.

New Possibilities

Still, empowering mayors and others whose worlds are wider than public education can open up new possibilities. They can introduce ideas from fields unfamiliar to public education professionals. They can also change the political calculus surrounding schools so that proposals once ruled out of the question can be entertained. New participants and even the trauma of takeovers breathe new life into the possibility of education reforms that include deregulation, weakening of union monopolies, competition among schools, and family choice.

There are other reasons to believe that changes previously thought impossible may now be feasible. Because most big city school districts have aging teaching forces, many will lose more than half their teachers to retirement in the next five years. At the same time, districts already replace or reassign one-third of their principals annually. Rapid staff turnover creates stresses, but it also opens up the possibility of recruiting potential teachers from different sources, hiring them under different conditions, building different work environments, and backing up redefined jobs with new forms of on-the-job training.

Equally important, major changes are afoot outside the schools. New coalitions of African-American ministers and grassroots leaders are demanding educational reform in many cities. The Supreme Court's failure to overturn Milwaukee's voucher plan when offered the possibility also opens up the chance that public education in cities can be provided by nonprofit groups. Charter schools are increasingly seen in Chicago, Rochester, New York, and elsewhere as ways cities can provide choices for needy students.

Whether these opportunities for change lead to anything different— and whether changes adopted lead to improvements in urban public education—depends on the new parties' ability to design, execute, and stick with powerful reform strategies. If mayors and others who assume responsibility for city school reform continue cycling through a series of poorly implemented reforms, or try to please all the educational interest groups by doing a little of one thing here and a little of something else there, the policy churn will continue.

Today's mayors, civic and foundation leaders, and school boards must construct strategies that are more powerful, more coherent, longer lasting, and more completely carried through than past efforts. However, they cannot be made out of whole cloth or constructed in ignorance of the problems of schools. Like new management teams taking over troubled businesses, mayors and others need to learn about school reform issues without letting themselves be drawn into internecine struggles within the education establishment.

Main Competing Proposals

The urban reform struggles revolve around seven competing policy approaches identified and analyzed in *Fixing Urban Schools.*[9] The first four describe reform as prescribed and led from the inside. The last three provide a vision of reform conceived and perhaps imposed from without.

Standards

Standards proponents urge state and local leaders to establish clear and ambitious expectations about what students should know and be able to do. They also urge states to build a system of tests, curricula, teacher training, and teaching materials, all carefully aligned with the standards, and attach real consequences to test results for schools, students, and individual teachers. (For example, failing schools might be subject to state takeover, students might be retained in grade, and teachers' salaries might be tied to student performance.)

Standards-based reform assumes that clarity about what must be taught and learned will create demand for improvements in educational methods, focus teachers' efforts on instruction, and motivate parents and students to strive for better performance. Students will learn because their goals will be clear. The standards-based system is espoused by leaders such as Marc Tucker of the National Center on Education and the Economy and Marshall Smith, formerly at Stanford University and the University of Wisconsin, who served through 1999 as acting deputy secretary in the U.S. Department of Education.

Teacher Development

The teacher development strategy encourages policymakers to invest in teacher-controlled efforts to master subject matter and devise new methods of instruction. Reform based on teachers' professional development assumes that those who take responsibility for their own learning and practice will become more effective in the classroom, the spirit of innovation will engage those whose practice is now stagnant, teacher-developed methods will be of higher quality than those created by nonteacher developers, and teacher excitement about improved practice will drive reform of public school systems. Students will learn because their teachers will be energetic, well prepared, and engaging. Prominent advocates of this approach include Linda Darling-Hammond of Stanford

University, Governor James Hunt of North Carolina, and the leaders of both major teacher unions.

New School Designs

The idea of new designs is appealing in its straightforwardness: help every school implement a comprehensive schoolwide design based on a particular approach to pedagogy—for example, teach via student-initiated projects or use computer-based instruction or study and discuss great books. Design-based reform assumes that schools that use a defined and consistent approach to instruction will be more focused and consistent, teachers will work together more productively, and parents and students will fully understand what the school promises and what is required of them. It also assumes that effective designs for integrating whole schools around an instructional strategy will be picked up and used by schools and districts. Students will learn because their schools are organized to provide consistent high-quality instruction and to remedy teaching and learning failures as they occur. School designs have been championed by the business community through the New American Schools Development Corporation and by the former deputy secretary of education and chairman of the Xerox Corporation, David T. Kearns.

Decentralization and Site-Based Management

The animating idea of decentralization is the conviction that schools are overregulated by bloated district staffs. Advocates argue for providing new decisionmaking responsibilities for teachers and parents, often in conjunction with reducing the size and powers of the central office. Decentralization-based reform assumes that greater school engagement in decisionmaking will encourage teachers and principals to take the initiative in rethinking both their instructional methods and their relationships to families and neighborhoods. It also assumes that parents will become more engaged in their children's schooling, teachers and parents will work together to overcome home and neighborhood factors interfering with teaching and learning, and students will learn because parents and neighbors, who understand and support the schools' efforts, will not tolerate lax performance by students or teachers. The most prominent experiment in decentralization in the United States in recent years was the 1989 reform developed in Chicago.

Insiders' Baseball

Each of the four strategies we have described—standards, professional development, school designs, and decentralization—enjoys the support of powerful political constituencies in the education community. An emphasis on standards, embraced by state agencies, corporate spokesmen, and political leaders interested in education, enjoys the wary support of teachers and local administrators. (Who, after all, can be seriously opposed to standards?) Teacher development, the brainchild of schools of education and teachers' union officials, is acknowledged to be a significant educational need by business and policy leaders. The new school designs, developed out of corporate America's experience in redesigning itself to meet foreign competition, enjoy the support of educational visionaries of all persuasions, who are convinced that, at long last, their theories for school improvement have found a congenial home. And while decentralization and site-based decisionmaking might be the bane of a school administrator's existence, the approach has been enthusiastically hailed by teachers' unions as a means of ridding the classroom of the meddling of officious central offices. In short, there is someone, somewhere in the interest groups surrounding education, in favor of each of these approaches—and often several someones.

But although each of the four proposals is modestly different from the others, the differences are more apparent than real. The standards-based approach (accompanied by its emphasis on alignment of tests, curriculum, teacher training, and curriculum materials to the standards) appears to be the most comprehensive, but the other three also require all-encompassing reform.

Teachers, after all, require development around something—standards, assessments, curricular competence, and the like, in fact around all of the things involved in standards-based reform. A serious effort at implementing new school designs or site-based management likewise requires rethinking everything about the school, root and branch. It is clear from the experience of school districts across the country that are carrying out the whole-school designs developed by the New American Schools

Development Corporation that even with a fully conceived design in hand, school districts and schools have been paralyzed by the scope of the educational decisions they needed to make. They still require an enormous amount of hand-holding and guidance from the experts who had developed the designs.[10] Turning to whole-school designs, teacher development, or site-based management has proven no panacea to avoid the complexity of the standards-based reform movement.

Because of these similarities, most of the proponents of the four strategies have little difficulty making common cause with each other. Indeed, in any educational conclave a sort of endless circularity is in evidence. Like the cook who wishes he had some eggs (because he could then make ham and eggs, if only he had some ham), educational theory seems forever trapped in a perpetual loop of needing something else. It wishes it had assessments, because then it could assess educational standards, if only it had standards, which should be tied to the curriculum, yet to be developed, which teachers then need to be trained to teach.

The perpetual circularity of this discussion, the philosophical predicate of policy churn, explains why educators can move from one policy discussion to another barely missing a beat, or even much modifying what they had intended to say. Because each of the major topics—standards, assessment, teaching, curriculum, school designs, and administrative structures—is enduring and significant, it is safe to enter the conversation at any point and, in effect, change the subject. The conversation is so circular that nobody notices. And the phenomenon is so familiar that nobody objects.

But the same cannot be said of the three remaining strategies described in *Fixing Urban Schools*: charter schools, contracting, and vouchers. For here, the frame of reference for the reform discussion is so radically new that everyone in the education community notices.

Charter Schools

Charter advocates promote authorizing schools to operate independently as long as they get good results for students, abide by public rules about equity of student admission and financial accounting, and allow parents to choose among schools. For the most part, charter supporters have called for a limited number of such schools in a district or a state, although the total number is increasing fairly rapidly. Thirty-six states (plus the District of Columbia) have now authorized over 1,000 schools nationwide. Charter schooling assumes that the opportunity to innovate will unite parents and teachers, that schools of choice will become strong communities, and that rivalry between charter schools and regular public schools will lead to demand for more widespread innovation and school freedom. Students will learn because schools will be specialized to meet particular needs and will strive to be considered highly effective. Support for charters, originally advocated by Ted Kolderie at the University of Minnesota, was limited at one time. It is now so broad and bipartisan that President Clinton did not hesitate to support a federal program to help encourage the establishment of 3,000 charter schools in his 1997 State of the Union address.

School Contracting

School contracting would create school-specific performance agreements that give schools complete control over their funds and staffing as long as they deliver promised curriculum and instructional methods, allow families to choose the schools their children attend, and see that students meet performance goals. It is the charter concept expanded districtwide. In some ways contracting can be understood as mandatory site-based management with parental choice and performance requirements tossed in. Contracting assumes that school independence and competition for students will encourage the search for more effective methods of instruction and that family choice will strengthen schools and family-school bonds. Students will learn because competition will force every school to focus its work on an explicit theory of teaching and learning, and parents will be able to select schools that match their children's interests and learning styles. Advocates include the authors of this book, along with James Guthrie of Vanderbilt University and Lawrence Pierce, recently retired from the University of Washington. Former Department of Education Deputy Secretary David T. Kearns and his colleague James Harvey have also supported contracting tied to national standards development.

Vouchers

Advocates of vouchers would eliminate direct public funding of schools in favor of giving vouchers to parents to be redeemed for tuition at any school. Voucher proposals assume that freeing up demand will attract high-quality independent school providers and drive innovation, and that choice will allow families to select schools they trust and can support. Students will learn because competition will favor schools that are productive and responsive and eliminate schools that provide ineffective instruction. Voucher advocates envision all the benefits of the market—competition and the ability to comparison-shop for quality—with few of the drawbacks, including false advertising and consumer fraud. Vouchers have attracted an eclectic mix of proponents from conservative economist Milton Friedman in the 1960s to progressive reformers, including former Milwaukee school superintendent Howard Fuller, in the 1990s.[11]

Outsiders' Pressure

What unites these last three proposals is that each has been advanced by reformers outside the education establishment. One finds very few stalwarts from schools of education advocating charters, contracting, or vouchers. Educators have given ground grudgingly on charter schools, but even here it is clear that pressures within the system unite to reimpose on charter schools the very regulations their charters were intended to rid them of.[12] What is clear is that, disenchanted with the possibilities of genuine reform from within, people outside the education system have intensified the pressure for more radical and fundamental change.

Insiders rally to many familiar flags when under assault by proponents of charters, contracting, or vouchers. Insiders are inclined to argue that providing funds outside the system will weaken public education, as though public education is the system and not the public that supports it and whom it is supposed to serve. At the extreme, educators will argue that this is "our money." They also point to the untried nature of these proposals. Archly inquiring as to how accountability is to be ensured, they conveniently ignore the lack of accountability that characterizes public education today. More thoughtful critics of these proposals worry about how the function of the traditional public school as social unifier will be passed on in an era of charters, contracts, or vouchers. This is a serious concern that requires a serious response from outsiders.

Efficacy of the Seven Proposals

In *Fixing Urban Schools* the authors analyzed each of the seven proposals from the point of view of their strongest supporters, asking, "if this initiative worked exactly as you expect, how would it lead to better schools and increased student achievement?" We learned that there is a plausible case for each of the proposals; each addresses a real problem and would probably cause real changes in public education if fully implemented.

But we also found that none of the proposals was sufficient because none could deliver all of the changes its proponents intended unless other changes, which the proposal itself could not deliver, occurred at the same time. For example, reforms based on teacher training do not create incentives to overcome some teachers' reluctance to put in the time and effort to improve their knowledge and skills. In a similar vein, reforms such as vouchers do not in themselves guarantee that there will be a plentiful supply of high-quality independent school providers or that enough teachers and principals qualified to run such schools exist. As *Fixing Urban Schools* concluded, every one of the major education reform proposals has a "zone of wishful thinking" in which its proponents assume but do not provide for complementary changes in individuals and society.

The earlier book also showed that the major proposals have complementary strengths and weaknesses. Proposals such as teacher training lack strong performance incentives, which vouchers and contracting provide aplenty. Marketlike proposals such as contracting lack major investments in teacher and administrator capacity, but teacher training and new school designs encourage just these features. Standards and new school designs, by contrast, provide useful information about desired practices and outcomes, but they rarely set out to create flexibility for educators in highly regulated urban schools so that the manner in which time, staff, and resources are used can be changed.

Three Essential Elements

Fixing Urban Schools concluded that none of the major proposals could by itself transform schools and student learning, but that hybrid reforms, combining the strengths of different proposals, were more promising and likely to be more powerful. It also suggested a way of thinking about how to build and assess the potential value of hybrid proposals. Every systemwide reform strategy must have three strong and interdependent elements: *incentives for school performance, ways of increasing school capabilities,* and *opportunities for school staff to change how they serve students.*

These elements must work together. If a strategy includes incentives, every adult's performance matters. This element encourages schools in which students learn because the people who work in them are rewarded, and children are removed from situations in which they are not learning. If a strategy includes increasing school capabilities, the school's capacity to function in its basic role is enhanced. The community invests in new ideas, new methods of instruction, teacher training, and recruitment of new teachers. Schools get help devising improvement plans and assessing their progress. And communities insist schools fill teacher vacancies with the best available people, not just those who are on the top of the civil service transfer list. If a strategy increases opportunities for school freedom, creativity is encouraged to blossom. School leaders and teachers, relieved of rules that limit instruction and make it routine, are free to use staff and money in innovative ways.

Just as all three features must work together, all three are essential. Each reinforces the others. Incentives highlight the importance of performance, investing in capacity building raises aspirations, and freedom removes the excuses for failing to strive for high standards. Policymakers who hope to reform schools by prescribing one or two of the features while neglecting the third will be entering simply another zone of wishful thinking and setting themselves up for more policy churn.

After reviewing these seven major proposals for transforming public education, *Fixing Urban Schools* concluded that there is broad agreement about how the environment for teaching and learning must change. The reform proposals all intend to make urban schools simpler, more focused places where adults share ideas about good teaching and where teachers and parents share responsibility for children's learning and well-being.

Taken together, existing reform proposals might be joined together in effective strategies that combine opportunities for changes in the ways schools are staffed and run, incentives for educators to seek improvements and change their routines, and capabilities for higher performance based on proven ideas about instruction and school management.

At present, however, these initiatives are not taken together. Combined strategies that draw from the strengths of diverse reforms are prevented by rivalries and cultural gaps among reformers. Rival groups of academics and reform promoters think they own the intellectual and moral high ground and that proposals competing with their own would have disastrous consequences.

Effective big-city reform strategies are possible. But many things must change. Scholars who invent and advocate reform ideas must adopt principles of truth in advocacy. Foundations and businesses that support local reform efforts must adopt the discipline of cause and effect thinking and refuse to be captured by ideas that are too one-sided to work. Local authorities, including mayors, school boards, superintendents, and civic leaders, must resist adopting feel-good and quick-fix reforms and commit to hard-nosed evaluation and continuous strengthening of reform initiatives.

Those were difficult conclusions to reach at the time. They have not become easier to contemplate since the book was published. But our conviction that one-size-fits-all reforms cannot work and our commitment to hard-nosed evaluation and continuous strengthening of local initiatives has only increased since *Fixing Urban Schools* was published. For the lessons we have learned in six cities make it clear that unless policymakers outside the schools insist on powerful new formulations to improve school and student performance, our cities and their citizens will continue to be the victims of what amounts to policy churn and educational quackery: quick-fix reforms that accomplish little, but leave the public more cynical about its schools after the good feeling accompanying their implementation has disappeared and nothing has changed.

Lessons from Six Cities | 2

H OW CAN MAYORS and other leaders construct reform strategies that promise to be powerful enough and last long enough to make a difference? That question lies at the heart of this volume. We started to seek an answer by examining how significant, well-regarded, nationally applauded reform efforts had fared in six major cities. We present the results of that examination in broad descriptive strokes here; in the next chapter we analyze what happened in each of these six cities and add to the analysis the major findings from our simulation exercise in three communities. Together, these two chapters provide a picture of how various reform initiatives fare in the field and how local leaders and citizens comprehend the possibilities for reform.

Our main source of data was intensive case studies of six cities that had gained national reputations as places trying out bold and promising new ideas for citywide education reform. Although the six displayed some similarities, in essence each provided a different story, both about the manner in which reform was approached and how the effort developed.

City Case Studies

Based on nominations from knowledgeable researchers and educators, we chose Boston, Memphis, New York (School District 2), San Antonio, San Francisco, and Seattle for close study. Each had initiated an ambitious reform plan intended to make dramatic improvements in the performance of all public schools. As we started the study in mid-1997, each of the cities had a widely respected plan for school improvement that was backed with strong leadership and community support.

Synopses of each district's reform efforts follow.[1] Teams of researchers visited each city twice for an average of eight days, interviewing superintendents, district administrators, principals, teachers, union leaders, school board members, business and civic leaders, and university researchers. The teams also analyzed official documents about reform plans and budgets and studied recent reports, evaluations, and newspaper and journal articles. The issues we explored included

—what each person interviewed thought the district's reforms to be and how broadly shared they were;

—how initiatives taken at the district level were expected to result in improvements in teaching and learning;

—what political, financial, and practical obstacles had arisen and how these were overcome; and

—whether the reform could be sustained if the superintendent left.

These cities' experiences are the raw materials we will use throughout this book. Although leaders in other cities can get useful ideas simply by learning what these cities attempted, they can learn even more by looking across the sites and considering why the cities pursued different initiatives, where they have succeeded, where they are still struggling, and why.

Boston: Expectations and Support Lead to Improvement

Boston civic leaders recruited Superintendent Thomas Payzant to lead a fundamental reform of the city's public school system. He came to Boston in 1995 having already built a noteworthy career as a superintendent in three major cities and as assistant secretary for elementary and secondary education at the Department of Education. When Payzant arrived in Boston, political, business, and union leaders came together to back him and the idea of education reform. The state had recently enacted academic standards stating what every child should be expected to know and be able to do. Site councils for every school (groups of teachers, parents, and staff who develop each school's improvement plan) were in the works. In addition, the Annenberg Foundation had given Boston Public Schools a matching grant of $10 million to further develop a pilot project of Whole School Change in all schools. Through this model, schools choose an instructional focus (a specific schoolwide approach to teaching and assessment of student learning) and work with a coach to use student performance data to steer their spending and staff decisions in the hope of improving teaching and learning. Payzant built the Boston reform strategy to be a merger of both the state standards-based reform and the Annenberg-funded Whole School Change model. He intended to combine high performance expectations and intensive help for existing schools, and he expected that together these initiatives would improve student learning citywide.

Reform in Boston has just begun, but the city has all of the fiscal, human, and political resources in place for major systemic reforms. Boston Mayor Thomas Menino has taken the rare stance of resting his political legacy on the success of the city's schools and appointed the current school board, which hired Payzant. In three years Boston public schools have developed student achievement standards, an accountability policy that singles out poorly performing schools for special attention, and the innovative Whole School Change model based on instructional focus and strategic spending and staffing. The superintendent and central office are focused on the core mission of improving teaching and learning. Perhaps more important, they are self-reflective and willing to adapt.

Despite these early successes, Boston faces some major challenges. The first is to match the time, money, and energy available to school staff with the actions required by the city's reform initiatives. The second is to ensure that educators in the system are well qualified, well trained, and well supervised. This will be crucial to implementing the reforms and addressing the district's student performance goals. Finally, time is a challenge. If test scores have not significantly improved in three years (when

Menino is up for reelection), his opponent might use that failure against him. Should the mayor be defeated, the current reform effort would probably unravel and the system would be faced with the likelihood of a new superintendent bringing a new wave of reform.

Boston has to balance the measured pace necessary to bring the entire system along with the need to establish the credibility of this reform quickly. The conditions for reform in Boston represent a brief window of opportunity.

Memphis: Importing Intellectual Capital

Superintendent Gerry House came to Memphis in 1992 and promptly initiated a communitywide strategic planning process for school reform. The resulting plan centers on high achievement for students and increased accountability for adults. In addition to incorporating community ideas, the plan is aligned with the Tennessee Education Improvement Act. The act legislated new standards, accountability systems, school-based decisionmaking, more staff development, annual assessments and exit tests, and a new funding formula that provides more funds to poorer counties with lower rates of local support.

The Memphis school district is confronted with high poverty rates, consistently poor student performance on the state's standardized tests, and few fiscal resources available to tackle problems. House looked outside the district for new tools and resources. In particular, she recommended the use of whole school design models such as those provided by the New American Schools Development Corporation—curriculum and training packages that all Memphis schools have now chosen from to guide their schoolwide change. House further added systemic reform that supports carrying out the new designs. These include a new Teaching and Learning Academy designed to focus and increase professional development throughout the district, building the skills of current teachers to teach to new standards. She also increased accountability for principals, which has become a major force driving the reforms. More than half a principal's evaluation rests on student improvement on the state and district assessment tests. Failure to show improvement courts dismissal. The district has high performance expectations but has expressed willingness to be flexible in almost all other areas. Schools may request waivers from state or district policies if they impede innovations, though few have taken advantage of these possibilities.

What has happened to date? Five years after adoption of the strategic plan, Superintendent House can point to achieving many of its goals, developed with the participation of staff, students, parents, and community members. She enjoys a supportive board, the district has increased spending on professional development for all staff, and test scores of schools using the whole school designs showed a 14.5 percent gain over comparable Memphis city schools (without designs) at the end of the 1997–98 school year. These accomplishments lay behind House's selection as 1999 superintendent of the year by the American Association of School Administrators.

Now that the idea of whole school designs has been proven in principle, it must be applied in practice so that it affects all schools, not just those most open to change.

The reform faces two threats. First, many teachers and school office staff are skeptical that any educational improvement can benefit Memphis's poorest children. Second, many potential critics are quietly waiting to see whether the initiative will increase test scores dramatically enough to maintain teacher support. This is an especially sensitive issue because many teachers and principals say they are exhausted by all the extra work imposed by the citywide reform initiative and feel underappreciated. If scores do not continue to rise, House may lose the energy and the commitment of the teachers and principals who currently power the reform.

New York City District 2: Focus on Instruction

Anthony Alvarado served as superintendent of District 2 for more than a decade before recently moving to San Diego to be the new chancellor of instruction. His lengthy tenure in New York was remarkable because he was able to initiate and carry out school reform with a consistency few districts have been able to match. His plan has been to focus on instruction and make the mission of each school to be about one thing only—student learning.

To do this the district simplified rather than lowered reform expectations. Alvarado focused the district on teaching and learning. District 2 strives to be an "adult learning system," and professional development takes many forms. Master teachers and consultants work with individual teachers, peer networks and visits allow for collaboration, classroom support follows training, and assistant superintendents visit each school and every classroom twice a year. All of this professional development is geared toward the district's emphasis on strengthening literacy. District 2 has focused on literacy for more than seven years, directing all the available fiscal and human resources toward improving the reading and writing of its students.

The key to supporting this teaching and learning environment, Alvarado believed, was good principals. He drew his principals from within the system, aiming for them to be strong instructional leaders first and good administrators second. The principal's job, according to Alvarado, is to hire good people and know whom to counsel out of the system when professional development efforts have been unsuccessful.

The district has enjoyed some noteworthy successes. A focused and sustained effort, the reform has had a decade in which to become institutionalized. Clear roles and responsibilities at the district and school levels have helped systemic improvement. Grounded and focused professional development provides more effective support than random workshops. The district now has the second highest mathematics and reading scores in New York City. With Alvarado's departure, however, comes the question of whether the reforms can be sustained. His replacement, Elaine Fink, was his right hand for many years, so there is a good chance that the reforms will continue.

But there are other limitations to the replicability of the district's initiative in other cities. This reform strategy has occurred in a small elementary and middle school district within a large city and under the leadership of an exceptionally skilled and veteran administrator. Teachers and principals who did not want to work within Alvarado's framework could readily transfer to other New York City districts. Therefore, can the components of this plan be equally successful in a different city with different leadership? Can this approach work equally well in high schools? And, can it be sustained in District 2 without a nationally recognized school leader who was able to work the New York system to benefit his district?

San Antonio: Coaching for School Improvement

Superintendent Diana Lam came to San Antonio in 1994, taking the helm of an impoverished, poorly performing district. Nearly half of its ninety-five schools were on a list for state mandated takeover. Almost at once, she set about enacting sweeping reforms that were both controversial and potentially successful.

Lam made it clear when she became superintendent that the district's reform package would focus on instruction as she made major organizational changes and sought external resources to fund improvements. She reduced the layers of central administration and eliminated many small programs. With the money saved, she created school-based instructional guides, people selected for their knowledge about best instructional practice and their ability to work with teachers to improve classroom teaching. To bring comprehensive change to every school, she required every school to adopt New American Schools design, and promised three years's funding. Concerned that not every design emphasizes the acquisition of basic skills, she also introduced curriculum changes to address weaknesses in teaching and learning. Lam extended the school calendar to a modified year-round schedule, allowing teachers and students more time to master subjects. In addition, she embraced the legislature's accountability and testing initiatives as ways to push the district forward. She closed one failing high school and reopened it with a new staff and instructional program, all without encountering major challenge; but when she set about initiating a similar change for the district's faltering flagship high school, she ran into trouble. The move was so unpopular that it may have proved to be her undoing in San Antonio. The school board bought out the final years of her contract in late 1998; by mid-1999 Lam was headed to Providence, Rhode Island, to assume her fourth superintendency.

San Antonio, once a stagnant district, has been revitalized. The New American Schools designs, the creation of instructional guides, and the extended school calendar focus every school on instructional improvement and provide real opportunities for making it happen.

But political strife is challenging progress. Disagreements between the Lam administration and various members of the school board changed the amount of support for various innovations, including the financial support needed to pay for them. Friction with the board and one of the teachers' unions caused the board to buy out her contract. Some reforms, notably school designs and instructional guides, have been well received by school staff, but even these reforms have not yet been institutionalized. The board is also looking for ways to cover a funding shortfall, and Lam's various initiatives are being examined as likely candidates for cuts. The future of the reform effort in San Antonio remains uncertain.

San Francisco: Rebuild Failing Schools

Superintendent Waldemar Rojas based school reform in San Francisco on reconstitution: closing failing schools and requiring all staff to reapply for their positions. A court-ordered consent decree in 1982 required the district to desegregate schools through busing and to improve student achievement in impoverished neighborhoods through careful planning, infusion of funds, and reconstitution. Currently, schools are supported by a generously funded professional development program, focused budget priorities, and an extensive database that measures the results. Schools that demonstrate their ability to educate all students retain their autonomy. Schools that do not are targeted for reconstitution, a process dreaded by principals and teachers. Many schools have been reconstituted, although the first ones received the most planning and attention and, not surprisingly, were most successful. The district now faces the dilemma of what to do with reconstituted schools that are not successful.

The strengths of school reform in San Francisco include the clarity and single-mindedness of the goal, accompanied by a clear process and timeline for achieving it. Many schools have been targeted for reconstitution, and twenty-two have experienced it. After rebuilding the original group of six schools, however, other schools received only a watered-down version of support, technical assistance, and planning. Schools rebuilt in these subsequent phases are not achieving as well as the first group. Maintaining the credibility of reconstitution as a serious threat to business as usual remains a major challenge facing San Francisco.

In addition, a group of minority parents sued the district to end ethnic quotas that require their children to be bused to schools outside their neighborhood. The trial was heard by the judge who had ordered the original consent decree, and he found that the district has been successful at ending segregation. The district could now lose a significant portion of funds allotted for the purpose of obeying the decree. Recent board elections resulted in the loss of a strong supporter of the superintendent and the election of a member who is opposed to many reforms that Rojas and the board majority thought were important. Moreover, Rojas himself recently left San Francisco for the superintendency in Dallas. These events suggest that the next few years will be the most challenging yet for the supporters of San Francisco's reform initiative.

Seattle: Principal Empowerment

The late retired general John Stanford became superintendent of the Seattle Public Schools in 1995. Elements of school reform were under way before his arrival, but Stanford instituted unique ideas regarding school funding and leadership.[2]

He placed great emphasis on the importance of leadership at the school level, and developed a model of "principals as CEOs" of their schools. Principals are now charged with improving student test scores, solving problems in their schools, building good relationships with staff, developing resources, and conducting community and business outreach in a new era of competition for funds and students (whose parents have limited but real choices among schools).

In addition, principals are expected to manage the development of their budgets and the hiring of new teachers. To support these new responsibilities, Stanford set out to remove impediments to their success. He worked with union leadership to broker a new teacher contract, a "trust agreement" that removed the automatic right of senior teachers to choose the schools in which they teach. Principals can now create a cohesive team of teaching professionals and work to resolve conflicts in-house. Stanford and his staff also developed a weighted student formula designed to get more funding to schools with disadvantaged students. In exchange for flexibility, he expected increased student achievement on state and district tests and set new standards at the district level: students must pass "exit exams" in grades 5, 7, and 11 and have at least a C average to graduate from high school.

At the time of John Stanford's death from leukemia in the fall of 1998, the Seattle School District had built excitement and support, including significant private gifts and public funding. Nevertheless, a coherent strategy for reform had not been well defined. Some elements, such as the weighted student formula and school-level decisionmaking, may continue. Still, the greatest threat to these reforms is that very little has been institutionalized or made noticeable in the classroom.

New Superintendent Joseph Olchefske, a businessman whom Stanford hired as chief financial officer, has pledged to continue Stanford's work, but there is some question about how Olchefske will define that work. Teacher unrest over salaries and a mid-1999 change in union leadership from Roger Erskine, architect of the trust agreement, to a group committed to more aggressive collective bargaining, also create uncertainty. The new superintendent will almost surely have the same difficulty Stanford had in connecting the reforms into a coherent strategy to be understood by those at all levels of the district and in the community.

The Challenge of Implementation

Staff of the Center on Reinventing Public Education studied these cities to find ideas that others might use and discovered many useful concepts, as chapter 3 demonstrates. However, as will also be shown, few if any of the six cities' reform strategies were rigorous or complete enough to bring about all the improvements in schools that their initiators had anticipated. The strategies all had promise; if rigorously pursued for a decade or more, all might have made a greater difference than they did. For every city, however, a gap existed between the strategy's potential and its accomplishments. In each case the gap could be traced to problems of implementation, even in cities like Boston in which the reform was put in place without interruption.

First, we should acknowledge real implementation successes. New York City District 2 succeeded in reallocating a significant amount of money for instructional improvement and found ways of assigning unproductive and uncooperative teachers and principals to jobs outside the district. Boston, Seattle, and San Francisco gave schools access to financial and performance information in ways that increased schools' ability to plan. Seattle developed an unprecedented collaboration between district and union leadership (as had Rochester a decade earlier). Boston and Seattle attracted major private investments, while Memphis, San Antonio, and New York City District 2 brought in intellectual capital in the form of highly qualified staff developers and school design teams. San Francisco maintained for many years but ultimately lost major extra state funding that supported significant investment in school reconstitution. And San Antonio and Memphis both made significant use of outside school designs that created new opportunities for outstanding teacher leaders (as Cincinnati had done earlier). Memphis expanded the principal's responsibilities and Seattle announced (but has not yet fully put into operation) the intention to do so. Finally, Boston and Seattle built and maintained strong support from the mayor and business community.

Many reform strategies in other cities, including some that have by now been abandoned or profoundly changed, have also experienced major successes. These include developing strong teacher-principal collaborations in approximately one-third of district schools under a framework provided by local site councils (Chicago); creating new capabilities to track the progress of reform initiatives and conduct and report strong assessment of schools (Chicago); promoting formation of multiple providers of new schools (New York City); developing a small central office unit capable of selecting, managing, and evaluating a few schools run by independent providers (Chicago); and stimulating development of an infrastructure of nonprofit providers of assistance to schools (Charlotte, Los Angeles, and Ohio and Kentucky).

Problems That Plague Reform Implementation

The successes of the reform initiatives have been limited to particular aspects of a reform package or to a few schools. In most of the cities there have been offsetting failures: key elements of plans were never carried out or were carried out poorly. Political resistance, strikes, fiscal crises, scandals, emergencies affecting student safety, and dwindling public confidence in reform leaders have disrupted implementation and limited progress. The problems affecting big-city reform initiatives fall into the five categories shown in table 2-1.

Table 2-1. *Major Implementation Problems Affecting Education Reform Initiatives in Six Cities*

Problem	City
Loss of superintendent and disconnected succession	Seattle, San Antonio, New York City District 2 (also Charlotte, N.C.)
Weakening of support from board	San Antonio, San Francisco (also Charlotte, N.C.)
Teacher resistance	Memphis, San Antonio, San Francisco, Seattle (also Charlotte, N.C.)
Failure to sustain expected funding	Boston, San Francisco
Temporizing through delays, half-measures, and introduction of competing initiatives	Boston, San Antonio, San Francisco, Seattle, Memphis

At least one of these problems has interfered with reform implementation in every one of the cities. Optimists might see many of these problems as idiosyncratic to a particular city (political turmoil, for example, may be more severe in some cities than others) or as flaws in people's operating styles (Diana Lam's confrontational style or the abrasiveness that got John Murphy fired in Charlotte in 1995) or as sheer bad luck (General Stanford's illness and death in Seattle).

But over time virtually any local initiative is likely to encounter at least one of these problems. A local strategy that has not been designed to nail down indispensable funding or survive a superintendent's departure or buttress a superintendent's support against political challenges from school staff members who resent performance pressures is unlikely to last long enough to succeed.

Loss of a superintendent who was the originator of the reform strategy or had been its chief executor can obviously derail it. The loss can also understandably spread doubt among subordinate school system administrators, teachers, and principals, the people whose actions determine whether a reform strategy has any impact on schools and classrooms.

A disconnected succession in which a leading superintendent is replaced by another whose mandate is unclear does more than cast doubt. It makes clear that teachers and others who were willing to take initiative under the reform strategy cannot rely on support from above. It also opens reform supporters in schools and the central office to attack from opponents of reform. In every school system there are teachers, principals, and central office staff who dislike or resent the reform but decide to wait it out rather than to oppose it overtly. When opponents feel free to come out and attack reform supporters, an initiative is dead.

Death of a reform initiative at the hands of resurgent opponents is common: it happened to virtually every urban reform effort we have tracked in four study projects.[3] In the cities studied for this book such opposition appears to have been important in Seattle (due to the departure of teachers' union leader Roger Erskine and the abandonment of John Stanford's "Focus" strategy for low-performing schools) and in San Antonio (due to opposition to continued spending on New American Schools designs brought in by Diana Lam).

In cities studied earlier, Richard Wallace's close supervision of Pittsburgh school performance ended soon after his retirement. Dade County's commitment to rigorous devolvement of decisionmaking to schools and to the new Saturn schools incubator crumbled when the superintendent backing the reform, Joseph Fernandez, was succeeded by a central office insider. Chicago's 1988 initiative based on the formation of local site councils was fatally weakened when the school board appointed two superintendents in succession who did not consider implementation of the reform to be their first responsibility. Charlotte's commitment to superintendent-centered school performance agreements ended when a new superintendent committed to avoiding John Murphy's management style was appointed.

Weakening of board support for a reform can have the same debilitating effect on a strategy even if the superintendent is not fired. Weakening of the San Francisco school board's commitment to school performance oversight and reconstitution might have doomed the reform even if Rojas had not left the city. It is clearly possible for superintendents to survive while their reforms die.

Sometimes boards lose their focus on a reform strategy because they never truly understood it. That might prove to be true in Seattle, where board members agreed on their support for Stanford but might not have shared a clear picture of what he was doing. The old Chicago school board, before Mayor Daley's takeover of the school system in 1995, apparently never fully understood the reformers' intentions. This might also have doomed the late-1980s reform plan created by the Cincinnati Youth Initiative. Board incomprehension comes from two sources: superintendents' and other leaders' confidence that they can succeed without board support, creating such dramatic early successes that board members will not dare oppose them; and board members' avoidance of hard issues that might disrupt smooth working relations with each other. Whatever the source, a board's inability to comprehend the dimensions of the reforms it is supposed to oversee is fatal to an initiative that must be carried out over a long time (as all must) or encounters unexpected challenges (as all do).

Even when board members understand and strongly support a reform, support can be eroded by teacher opposition. Elections, and board members' need to anticipate them, are important mechanisms by which unhappy teachers can oppose a reform initiative. In any reform environment, even the best and most dedicated teachers will experience pressures for change. Learning new methods, spending more time deliberating with parents or other teachers, changing work schedules, working in differently configured classrooms or in less quiet and private surroundings, taking more personal responsibility for student progress, administering tests and openly discussing the implications of test results—all of these changes and others require major adjustments from teachers. Any reform meant to improve student learning will inevitably affect teachers and can potentially encourage teacher resistance.

Few teachers are likely to enjoy such pressures, and though many will accept them as necessary and desirable, significant numbers do not. Moreover, teachers who lose confidence that the superintendent and other reform leaders have a definite strategy are sure to resent initiatives imposed from above. Thus any important reform initiative, whether well or poorly carried out, is likely to elicit teacher opposition. If this opposition becomes organized, either through union-led actions or efforts to control school board elections, it can strongly affect board members. Traditionally, low turnout in school board elections creates real opportunities for a large, even semiorganized group to exert its will. Dissident teacher groups, sometimes led by unions and sometimes not, have helped derail reform initiatives in cities as diverse as Charlotte, Detroit, Milwaukee, San Antonio, and San Francisco.

On an even smaller scale, dissident groups within teachers' unions can weaken or fire reform-oriented local leaders: in the cities we have studied, Seattle's Roger Erskine and Cincinnati's Tom Mooney were both forced by internal dissidents to soft-pedal their work on reform.

Relying on highly optimistic estimates of extra funding can also open a trapdoor beneath reform. Funding shortfalls now threaten reforms in San Francisco and Memphis, as they did Dade County's, Houston's, and Charlotte's in earlier reform cycles. Most major initiatives require significant front-end investment, and many reform leaders are tempted to win the support of teachers and administrators by promising funding that they do not have but hope to get if they can claim early success. These tactics sometimes work, but they can be fatal to a reform if independent governments and philanthropists are not favorably impressed.

Competing initiatives put in place after a communitywide strategy is announced and not clearly reconciled with it disrupt implementation. "Strategy creep," a loss of clarity about what is being attempted and how, signals lack of focus or unanimity at the top. The resulting confusion can make things impossible for principals and teachers' union leaders who support the strategy. They cannot assure teachers and others that promised (or threatened) changes are coming. Nor can principals and union heads count on high-ranking leaders to back them against dissident colleagues and constituents.

Mixed signals are a constant problem in education reform. Many in San Antonio blame Superintendent Lam's downfall at least in part on teacher discontent caused by her announcement of a new staff training program before schools had completed the training required by the New American Schools designs. Lower-level administrators and teachers in most of the cities we studied knew when school boards were divided or when there were differences between superintendent and board. Stating a strategy clearly and staying on the message are major challenges in a turbulent urban education environment. Of all the reform leaders we studied, only New York's Alvarado and Memphis's House appear to have mastered it.

Temporizing through reliance on half-measures and delay is the most important implementation problem. It comes from efforts to avoid other problems—controversy, teacher opposition, concerns about costs, or criticism that an initiative is taking too much time. Only a few of the reform initiatives we have studied avoided the problem of half-measures. Highly touted reform initiatives—Rochester's commitment to greater teacher outreach; decentralization in Chicago, Denver, and Miami; equalization of teacher resources in Los Angeles; Seattle's per pupil funding; San Francisco's reconstitution; and Cincinnati's creation of a principal-led central office—have been compromised from the beginning.

Though some compromises were caused by dollar shortages, most have been politically driven. Facing opposition, reform leaders have quietly weakened their initiatives while keeping the names and performance promises intact. Thus in San Francisco the concept of school reconstitution was degraded from an earlier approach that involved complete re-thinking of school plans and staffing to a quick, constrained process designed to minimize inconvenience to teachers. In Seattle the commitment to sending additional dollars to a school for each student enrolled was shelved to protect central office control of more than half the budget and to protect schools whose teachers were all at the top of the district's pay scale. The results were to limit the effectiveness of the active ingredient (reconstitution) in San Francisco's school reform and to deprive Seattle's poverty-area schools of much of the extra funding they had been promised.

Delay is simply a variation of temporizing. It is often caused by re-form supporters' own advocacy strategies, just as funding shortfalls sometimes are. Many reform leaders avoid creating clear incentives and performance pressures, hoping that teachers and administrators will come on their own to appreciate and support a strategy for change. Many reformers also build support without making clear how much time it will take to assemble the administrative machinery, create the performance data on which incentive schemes depend, find training and assistance for people who are trying to learn new ways of working, and inform parents and voters about how the reformed system will work. The result is a reform strategy that will take years to develop.

Delays caused by unrealistic expectations threaten a reform initiative even when there is little organized opposition: superintendents, administrators, board members, mayors, business and community leaders, and foundation grant officers can all move, retire, or set new *career goals. New people must be brought on board, but if their predecessors say things are not moving as rapidly as they hoped (or if results are still out in some indefinite future), it may be impossible to gain new people's commitment. Initiatives can survive such transitions, but their doing so is risky. Long-acting reform initiatives such as Boston's, Seattle's, and San Francisco's (and before them those of Cincinnati, Los Angeles, Denver, and Philadelphia) are particularly vulnerable to these inevitable transitions.

Moving Ahead

Against the backdrop of the experiences of these six cities, it becomes clear that, at a minimum, civic leaders hoping to advance long-lasting and sustained educational reform must take these five lessons to heart. Making a difference will require developing strategies to address tenure and succession issues in the superintendency, provide for loss of nerve on the part of board members or political resistance from teachers, and cope with the inevitable human tendency to temporize, settle for delay, and hope to get by using half-measures, competing initiatives, or inadequate funding as excuses for inaction.

But serious reformers must do far more. The reality is that even if all these impediments are taken into account, most of the reforms under discussion are very thin gruel indeed. When we look beneath the surface of these efforts, what we find are weak treatments, unlikely to make much difference because their advocates place so much hope in outcomes that are difficult to achieve while ignoring blind spots in their own strategies.

Beneath the Surface: Theories of Action | 3

CHAPTER 2 described six cities' reform initiatives as examples from which leaders in other cities might learn. This chapter tries to increase the value of those experiences by comparing the strengths and weaknesses of each city's strategy and describing the theories of action that reform planners hoped would lead to school improvement. The chapter rounds out this analysis by arguing that leaders, citizens, and educators are willing to consider bolder and much more far-reaching reforms, as indicated by the results of decisionmaking simulations conducted with leaders in several cities, and concludes that combining different reform elements can create much more potent and meaningful strategies.

Comparing the Cities' Reform Initiatives

The six cases illustrate how numerous different reform elements are being employed in the sample cities. Table 3-1 compares these reform initiatives along ten dimensions. As the table makes clear, only two features are universal: the adoption of student performance standards and use of outside experts (not just central staff) for teacher in-service training.

Table 3-1. *Education Reform Initiatives in Six Cities*

Initiative	Boston	Memphis	New York District 2	San Antonio	San Francisco	Seattle
Student performance standards	Yes	Yes	Yes	Yes	Yes	Yes
School control of funds	Limited	No	Limited	No	No	Limited
School performance agreements	No	Yes	Yes	Yes	Yes	Yes
Hiring staff	No	No	Limited	Yes	Yes	Yes
Use of whole-school designs	No	Yes	No	Yes	No	Limited
Reconstitution	No	No	No	Yes	Yes	Once
Extra spending and non-routine initiatives to improve teachers' skills, basic knowledge	Yes	Yes	Yes	Yes	Yes	No
Use of outside vendors for professional development	Yes	Yes	Yes	Yes	Yes	Yes
Effort to attract teachers from new sources	Planned	Yes	No	Limited	Yes	No
New union agreements on work rules	Limited	No	No	No	Limited	Yes

Table 3-1 shows that none of the reforms drastically attempts to alter the control of funds at the school level. Although Seattle, for example, has devolved control of the budget to individual schools—they nominally control 55 percent—principals still do not have control of personnel funds. Lack of control for these funds hinders the principals' ability to make major changes in school expenditures.

Most of the districts have instituted school performance agreements, whereby schools must outline a plan of action for the year ahead, justify it by recent student assessment results, and refer to the agreement when making decisions regarding resource allocations. The consequences of not living up to these agreements, however, vary from district to district. In some these agreements, once made, are put aside, while in others they lead to greater district scrutiny and sometimes reconstitution.

Most of these districts have arranged to devolve hiring staff to the school level where principals or teams of teachers and administrators interview qualified candidates to choose those who best fit the needs of the school. This arrangement has been well received in these districts, though in most cases it is too early to determine whether schools are experiencing better teamwork or if the strategy has strengthened the teaching staff.

San Antonio and Memphis are both experimenting with districtwide whole school designs aimed at introducing coherent curriculum and staff development into every school. In both cities New American Schools make up most of the designs used, but both have other models in place as well. The jury is out as to whether the use of a schoolwide design has much impact on student learning, although local evaluations in the two cities report promising results. Anecdotal evidence in our case studies showed that principals and teachers who were involved in selecting their school designs believed strongly that they were of great value in channeling instruction to complement each successive grade level and providing each school with a focus. In addition, Seattle is using school designs in a limited way to improve poorly performing schools.

Reconstitution is a final serious step for districts that have made a firm commitment to accountability. Of the case study cities, San Francisco has been the most aggressive with this approach and has experienced mixed success. Reconstitution alone did not account for improvement in schools, but coupled with intensive planning, support, and follow-up, it appears to show that it can turn a school around. San Antonio has also experienced mixed successes, reconstituting one poorly performing high school, backing it up with support, seasoned administrators and educators, and close follow-up. This school made great gains in test scores only a year or two after the change. The next attempt at reconstitution, this time of a popular but educationally deteriorating high school, galvanized teachers and parents to react to such severe measures, and though the reconstitution was carried out, it was one of the reasons for the resignation of Superintendent Lam. Seattle reconstituted one poorly performing middle school, but the experience was fraught with inept leadership choices and unclear visions of what the school ought to be. It is doubtful that Seattle will undertake reconstitution again any time soon.

It is clear from table 3-1 that professional development and teacher training are receiving a lot of attention in every one of the six districts. Practically all report spending additional funds to improve teachers' skills and basic knowledge, and every district also turned to outside advisers to improve the professional development opportunities available.

Equally clear in each of the six districts is that there are few novel approaches to teacher recruitment or the renegotiation of union work rules. Although many suggestions have been made in recent years to encourage teacher recruitment from alternative sources—the private sector, government, military, or through alternative training programs for recent college graduates who have not taken enough courses in schools of education to be eligible for teaching certificates—only Memphis and San Francisco reported they were pursuing such a strategy. The other four cities were either uninterested or reported plans to adopt the strategy in the future. As table 3-1 shows, few districts have been able to change teachers' union work rules. Seattle reports it has developed new agreements with unions; Memphis, New York City District 2, and San Antonio state that they have not; and Boston and San Francisco reported limited changes.

Yet without basic changes in work rules, it is hard to understand how profound, deeply rooted change can be expected in any urban school system. These work rules are so complicated that they can impose sever constraints on schools' instructional programs.[1] Long-term union leaders and financial administrators involved in the negotiations are typically the only educators in the district with a full grasp of the history of these contracts. Some of the provisions, built frequently on memorandums of understanding between the district and the union, case law, and negotiated agreements, make up, in effect, "the contract behind the contract," said Fuller. Yet in the face of this powerful institutional anchor, only Seattle of the six districts has reported that it has negotiated changes in work rules, and those changes are trivial.

Analyzing the City Reforms

Figure 3-1 compares the cities' reform initiatives via the three-part framework introduced in *Fixing Urban Schools*. In reviewing the cause-

Figure 3-1. *Emphases of Six Cities' Education Reform Initiatives*

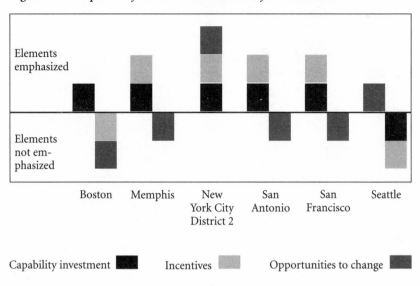

and-effect assumptions behind major reform proposals, the book concluded that all reform proposals could be reduced to three components: school performance incentives, investments in capacity, and school freedom of action. All the major reform proposals emphasize one of these components but are deficient in at least one of them. Reforms that emphasize teacher training often fail to create strong performance incentives. Reforms that emphasize performance incentives (the introduction of vouchers, for instance) often fail to provide for significant and carefully targeted investments in equipment, methods, and staff knowledge and skill. Reforms such as standards that leave the public education administrative structure in place fail to give schools the freedom of action necessary to replace unproductive uses of time and money with more effective ones.

This three-part framework of incentives, investments, and freedom of action is a simple way to compare reform initiatives and to summarize the different ideas about cause and effect that distinguish local initiatives from one another. Table 3-2 characterizes the six cities' reform initiatives in light of the framework. It shows that every city's initiative includes all three elements in some form, but it does not show whether

Table 3-2. *Elements of School Performance Incentives, Capacity Investments, and Freedom of Action in Six Cities' Education Reform Initiatives*

City	School performance incentives	Capacity investments	Freedom of action
Boston	School report card, "watch list," intervention teams	$25,000–$50,000 per school; coaches, university advisors	High-performing schools get charterlike autonomy
Memphis	Dismissal of principals in poorly performing schools	District-paid New American Schools teams	Waivers possible
New York City District 2	Transfer of poorly performing staff to other New York City districts	6 percent of budget spent on teacher learning; carefully selected assistance providers	Principals can change staff. 17 schools have "options"
San Antonio	Texas requires reconstitution of poorly performing schools	District-paid New American Schools teams; instructional guides, technology	Flexible school calendar, school choice of new teachers
San Francisco	Possibility of reconstitution	$40 million a year to aid desegregation; aggressive teacher recruitment	Limited school control of methods; some control over funds
Seattle	Limited family choice	Annual two-week principal training	School choice of new teachers, some spending discretion

the elements of any one city's reform initiative are equally strong, or for that matter whether the arrangements made for one reform element are well matched with other elements.

Table 3-2 shows that three strategies for rewarding or sanctioning performance were dominant in these cities: financial rewards for schools based on improvements along several dimensions, report cards encouraging public discussion of school performance, and threats of dismissal or reconstitution.

Financial incentives clearly drive the investment strategies, as one would expect; investments require resources. Here, funding for "coaches," leadership training, major attention to professional development needs, and support for outside expertise in the form of New American Schools designs are commonplace.

It is in support for school freedom of action that the reform efforts in the six cities appear most timid. School freedom of action involves deregulation: fewer requirements in return for improved performance. What we find in the six cities is not really deregulation at all, but opportunities for waiving regulations, all of which might be reimposed. Only in Seattle was a strong bias in favor of deregulation encouraged, but the encouragement rested largely on the charisma of the late superintendent and it is unclear whether it will survive the transition.

Different cities also emphasized different reform elements in their strategies. Figure 3-1 categorizes their approaches. Boston, Memphis, and San Antonio emphasize investments in new capabilities. However, none of the three provides unambiguous opportunities for schools to reorganize their staffs, budgets, or use of time, and Boston's reform does not provide strong rewards or penalties contingent on school performance.

What is clear from figure 3-1 is that, with the possible exception of New York City's District 2, none of the cities' reform initiatives is ideally constructed of three equally strong and mutually reinforcing elements. Later in this book, we examine District 2 in greater detail and ask about its value as an example: Can its strategy be reproduced without its combination of powerful and savvy leadership, ability to change staff, and easy availability of expert help?

Why is it that few districts have a strategy that balances incentives, investments in school capacity, and school freedom of action? The answer is probably that people start with what they know best: Thomas Payzant in Boston, a long-time educator, focused on investing in his staff; John Stanford in Seattle, a former army general, looked for unit leadership from principals and used his outsider's perspective to structure an exhortation to shake things up; Diana Lam in San Antonio brought in school designs with which she already had experience.

People also start with what is possible and avoid what is difficult and might put a stop to all progress. In San Francisco, Rojas started with reconstitution, which had a successful precedent in that city. Payzant and Stanford avoided strong performance-related incentives out of fear of teacher unrest. Effective reform efforts, however, will require stepping beyond these comfort zones.

Where the Reforms Are Now

Table 3-3 provides an overview of the challenges the reform initiatives face. Although all face challenges, most are definitely alive. Some are taking more time than expected, which is significant only in that it exposes them to doubts and challenges. Initiatives in Boston and Memphis have the leaders they started with, and they probably have the greatest chance of eventually making a real difference in student learning. These matters are discussed further in chapter 5.

Table 3-3 also shows our assessment, based on interviews throughout each school system, of whether the citywide or district policies that started the reform have led to actions that affect instruction and student learning. This is by no means a final judgment of any initiative, but it supports the idea that many have a long way to go and, even if on schedule, are a long way from reaching their ultimate goals.

Theories of Action and Zones of Wishful Thinking

The reform efforts in the six cities were diverse. One way to understand the differences is to compare the cause-and-effect assumptions on which the cities' strategies were based. What theories of action animated these reforms? What assumptions did district leaders make about what would happen in response to the changes they initiated? We answered this question by analyzing interviews with superintendents and other reform leaders, paying special attention to the reasons they expected their initiatives to cause changes in classroom instruction and increases in student learning. The results of this analysis are shown in table 3-4.

Teacher learning opportunities were the prime mover in Boston, new school designs in San Antonio and Memphis, and an activist super-

Table 3-3. *Status of Six Cities' Education Reform Initiatives, September 1999*

City	Biggest challenge	Pace of implementation	Effect to date on instruction and school performance
Boston	Will the superintendent accomplish reforms in time for the political promises at stake?	Slightly behind schedule	Little
Memphis	If test scores drop, will faculty and staff persevere with difficult reforms?	On schedule	Moderate
New York City District 2	Can it continue without the charismatic superintendent at the helm?	On schedule	High
San Antonio	Will board politics derail the reform after the resignation of the superintendent?	In abeyance— awaiting new superintendent	Moderate
San Francisco	Can the district return to reconstitution with intense support of schools?	In abeyance— awaiting new superintendent and financial implications of end of busing court order	Moderate
Seattle	Will the new superintendent be able to build on the general's record to create a mandate for coherent and aggressive action?	In abeyance— awaiting new superintendent's initiative	Little

intendent's insistence that the district had no priority other than instruction in New York City District 2. In San Francisco reform depended on reconstitution and monitoring of results and in Seattle on inspirational leadership and the attempt to create strong principals.

Table 3-4. *Assumptions behind Six Cities' Education Reform Strategies*

City	Assumption
Boston	Sustained investment in planning and training, publication of school test results, and efforts to create staff unity in every school motivate improvement
Memphis	Remodeling every school on a design developed elsewhere, coupled with central office monitoring of student test results, will motivate improvement
New York City District 2	Focusing all district-school transactions on instructional issues, providing assistance from expert vendors, close monitoring of student test results, and removing uncooperative or poorly performing staff will lead to improvement
San Antonio	Remodeling every school on a design developed elsewhere, placement of instructional coaches in every school, and threats to reconstitute poorly performing schools will lead to improvement
San Francisco	Close monitoring of individual school performance, increased spending, and shuffling staffs in poorest performing schools will lead to improvement
Seattle	Inspirational leadership, reallocation of some funds to low-income schools, and public discussion of the idea that principals have no excuses and should aggressively lead their schools will lead to improvement

All these assumptions are plausible. Many people, including the authors, think the logic behind District 2's strategy is particularly sophisticated. That does not mean, however, that the same logic could work in localities that might not be able to find a superintendent as capable of instructional leadership, as politically skillful, and as practiced in divesting the district of nonperforming staff as was Anthony Alvarado. District 2 does, however, provide proof of a school system that combines incentives, capacity building, and opportunity into an effective reform strategy.

Table 3-5 shows the strengths and weaknesses of the six cities' reform efforts from another angle. The analysis reflects an idea introduced in *Fixing Urban Schools*, the zone of wishful thinking. The table identifies

Table 3-5. *Zones of Wishful Thinking in Six Cities' Education Reform Strategies*

City	Zone of wishful thinking
Boston	Staff will change without significant contractual modifications. Change will come fast enough to maintain public support
Memphis	Schools will improve without clear freedom of action
New York City District 2	The most laggard schools will respond to the current combination of incentives, investments, and opportunities
San Antonio	Schools can sort among different demands for instructional change. Superintendent will survive confrontation with teachers' union
San Francisco	Schools can be reconstituted quickly and well through "expansion draft." Extra state funding will continue, and district's ability to sustain reconstitution will survive conflict with teachers' union
Seattle	School staffs will seize opportunity to change without major investments in training or school designs. Superintendent's personal prestige can be converted into action at the school level

the events that each city's reform initiative requires, but cannot cause, to happen. Some of these zones of wishful thinking are very important because wishes are often not fulfilled. San Antonio's and Seattle's reform designs were premised on their superintendents' continuation in office, yet by early 1999 Seattle's superintendent had died and San Antonio's had been pushed into resigning. San Francisco also lost its superintendent; in addition, it was in danger of losing its extra state funding for desegregation, and its reconstitution policy was under fire from new school board members.

A more detailed review of these and other cities' reform designs would identify additional forms of wishful thinking.

—Professional development opportunities affect teaching even in the absence of performance incentives.

—Principals and teachers will feel empowered by greater control of funds even if the amounts of funds they control are small.

—New policies will stimulate teachers to action even if school board support is tentative.

—Measurement and reporting of school performance will motivate improvement even if there is no link to consequences.

—School districts can figure out how to help all failing schools: there is no need to get outside advice.

—A work force of inadequate teachers can be transformed by retraining (terminations and new hires are not necessary).

—Reconstitution can lead to better schools even if new schools are assembled simply by picking a new staff from among teachers now employed by the district.

—Parents will be taken seriously even if they are not free to leave a school.

—Schools do not need greater freedom of action via deregulation: they can do whatever is necessary within the rules.

This presentation of unrealistic assumptions serves as background to a more important task, taken up in the next chapter, which is to create combined strategies that would be stronger than any one city's reform initiative. What if the strongest parts of different cities' reform designs were combined so that elements of wishful thinking were replaced by design elements that created strong school performance incentives, investments in school capabilities, and real school freedom of action?

Finally, as part of this stage-setting, we asked, "If leaders and the public could start afresh with reform, not with a completely blank slate, but with the basic system we have now, what kinds of changes would they be willing to entertain?" The answer is instructive.

Decisionmaking Simulations

The Brookings Institution and the Center on Reinventing Public Education created a simulation on school reform and hosted seven strategy-building simulations in Seattle, San Francisco, and Denver. These sessions aimed to engage reform innovators from different schools of thought in a neutral forum where they could work together to solve problems of public education and generate promising combinations of reform strategies that other innovators might be willing to investigate further.

Participants were invited to serve on a panel to advise the mayor of Edgeport, a hypothetical city facing serious public education problems. Simulation participants included professors of education and economics, superintendents, principals and assistant principals, education consultants, members of a business alliance and a nonprofit school reform organization, and mid-managerial professionals from a variety of public and private agencies.

Faced with a strict reform time line and pressure from the facilitator, panelists were forced to act quickly to gain agreement on their top three strategy recommendations to the mayor. In every case, rather than seek agreement on one best way to address the problems, the panelists' final recommendations included a combination of approaches to saving Edgeport's schools.

From these recommendations, three important conclusions can be drawn. First, all but one of the seven groups determined that both short- and long-term strategies were needed to turn the district around. Second, citing a lack of conclusive information about what works, several groups focused on the need for experimentation in designing a long-term strategy. Experiments involving charters and thorough deregulation won wide and fairly enthusiastic support. Finally, each panel's recommendations reflected a balance between centralized and decentralized power in the district. No panel recommended either a wholly centralized or decentralized approach to managing this failing district. In effect, the panels were trying to create a mix of central oversight of school performance harnessed to decentralized school control over expenditures, instructional methods, teacher hiring, daily schedules, and the like.

The simulations also recommended reform strategies that incorporated ideas going well beyond the strategies implemented in the six case-study cities.

—Let individual schools control 90 percent of all available funding, allocated on a per pupil basis.

—Start the reform planning process by demanding that the state waive all regulations and contracts.

—Make sure that student performance data are available for every student and school and can be analyzed by neighborhood, income, race, and gender.

—Create baselines to be able to monitor the value added by the reform initiative—districtwide and by school and student demographic group.

—Facilitate and insist on educators' discussion of school performance indicators and their implications for improvement efforts.

—Give parents choices among schools and make sure all parents get access to school performance information and help in learning how to use it.

—Let parents choose from all schools in the district.

—Avoid the political fallout from closing schools by creating accessible alternatives (for example, by chartering) and encouraging parents to choose them.

Many of these ideas will reappear in subsequent chapters as we consider bolder and potentially more effective reform designs. Beyond the ideas offered, the process and strategies used by the simulation participants reveal issues city leaders should also consider.

Process

The importance of a mixed group of people considering what to do cannot be overstated. Initially, most participants represented their real-life concerns and disciplines. Economists worried about how to use incentives to improve schools' performance. Educators focused on strategies that would increase the capacity of schools to serve students better (for example, professional development for teachers or cross-school sharing of best practices). In spite of these tendencies, however, the breadth of ideas considered by each group of panelists was impressive. Most expressed willingness to consider the perspectives of fellow panelists. Many acknowledged that they were operating solely on their hunches of what would work. As one participant explained, "There is no road map for us to follow to improve schools."

Many participants also agreed that they ultimately considered a much broader array of strategies than they had anticipated. They attributed their expansive thinking to the ideas of other panelists, who brought a variety of perspectives to the table.

Strategy

A combination of short- and long-term strategies was one of the consistent recommendations in many sessions. People agreed that, amidst crisis, both are needed, though the relationship between the two caused considerable debate. The central question: How to use a short-term strategy to increase test scores (and appease political concern) while simultaneously pursuing a coherent, long-term strategy that addresses the problems causing chronic underperformance?

Participants agreed that reform strategies can and should be combined into hybrid approaches—one-shot, specific strategies will not have the impact needed on deep-seated problems in the public education system. The specific combinations of strategies varied in each group.

The panels did not consider (and frequently did not raise) other reform strategies.[2] None was attracted to the idea of turning control of schools over to the state. Participants typically felt that state takeover was not an acceptable alternative. They spoke adamantly about the importance of retaining local control as a mark of local legitimacy and index of local pride. They also noted a lack of evidence that a state could run schools more effectively than local officials.

The groups spent little time considering a "great leader" approach. Typically, districts that rely on this strategy seek to recruit and retain a savvy, charismatic leader who can inspire schools to improve. In the best cases the person does just that, leaving the school district in a stronger position than when he or she arrived. Often, however, the successes fade once the leader has moved on. In the worst cases, hard-nosed evaluations of improvement under the great leader are muted because few people really want to learn that the great leader was anything less than great. Although some participants mentioned the importance of leadership in implementing a reform strategy, none appeared convinced that a great leader could solve every challenge of a district.

Finally, none of the panels spent much time trying to address the social and economic problems that might be contributing to the crisis of Edgeport's schools. Although one or two participants raised the idea of making schools more capable of meeting the health and social needs of low-income students, none advocated measures to address poverty, racism, housing shortages, or community violence that might place lasting school improvements beyond reach.

The panels' lack of emphasis on underlying social problems probably reflects several assumptions. The connection between school and community might not occur to many people. Others may have thought that educators cannot be permitted to use community conditions as an excuse for inaction. The panels may also have avoided these subjects because of doubts about society's willingness to do anything about them. Or they may have avoided them out of a deep belief (that did not need articulation) in the capacity of improved school systems to address the most pernicious problems in the long run. Fixing urban schools may still be the route to addressing income inequality and racism in the minds of these participants.

Creating More Robust Strategies

This chapter has provided the raw material for analysis in the chapters that follow. But how can communities combine these ideas into more robust, sustained, and powerful strategies? How can they make sure the reforms last long enough to work? How can cities now embarking on reform initiatives avoid the political and managerial pitfalls that have bogged down reform initiatives in the past and threaten some of the continuing reforms we have studied? These are matters we explore in the following chapters.

From Wishful Thinking to the Realities of Reform | 4

Fixing Urban Schools argued that genuine reform required more powerful strategies than have so far been employed, and it introduced the need for tripartite reform efforts that provided *incentives* for performance, *investments* in school capacity, and *deregulation*, or greater freedom and opportunity at individual schools.

This book broadens and deepens that analysis. It contends that policy churn and leadership turnover confound even the most highly regarded efforts to institutionalize reform efforts (chapter 1). It explores the challenges of implementation in six cities and from the experiences of those cities draws five challenges for civic leaders: the highly politicized nature of school governance, turnover in the superintendency, opposition from teacher unions or school boards, and the human tendency to hope that half-measures will suffice (chapter 2).

In chapter 3 we analyzed in greater detail the experiences in the six cities. We concluded that most reforms are logically incomplete because they create zones of wishful thinking by ignoring the need to address each element of the tripartite strategy. We also observed that, left to their own devices, educators, analysts, civic leaders, and members of the public almost spontaneously turn to more deep-rooted and potentially more robust reform strategies than the education establishment has been willing to consider. The simulation results discussed above indicate that lay people understand the need for short-term and long-term responses, endorse experimentation with radical ideas of deregulation and family choice, and are attracted to powerful district oversight of school performance tied to much greater freedom for schools to determine their own fates through control of budgets, hiring, and curricular emphases.

This chapter explores what reforms would look like if the most powerful elements of existing strategies were combined to create more powerful reform strategies. It insists that it is time to move from wishful thinking about how fine things will be when reform is finally achieved to hard assessments about the realities of what must be put in place to improve urban schools.

The goal of this chapter is to give city leaders ideas about reform strategies they might pursue. It goes beyond the efforts evident in the six cities to suggest strategies that would employ stronger combinations of incentives, capacity investments, and school freedom of action than any city has so far used.

The strategies actually used by the six cities were assembled by people who were familiar with a limited range of options and who had to bargain with one another about what was acceptable to different stakeholders. Leaders in our six cities were also pioneers: they had little basis on which to project the consequences of accepting a particular compromise or of leaving some things undefined, for example, consequences for continued poor performance or the likelihood of finding new sources of money for investment.

Despite some concerns about the untested nature of the alternatives we present, city leaders trying to turn around failed school systems should consider them. Not all are practicable everywhere, but a struggling city needs at least to look into them. A community that is deterred from considering bold options by interest group pressure or fear of the unfamiliar can never be sure that it has done everything possible for its children. What it can be sure of, unfortunately, is that it is well on its way to continuing the policy churn that has characterized urban schools for decades.

Reform Plans and Strategies

A reform plan is one or more actions intended to cause school improvement by changing one or more factors thought to affect school performance. A simple plan could be to increase spending, on the assumption that almost anything that could be bought with additional money would improve school performance. A more plausible plan would include some assumptions about cause and effect—for example that increased funding, combined with encouragement to use the new money to hire better-educated teachers, would improve school performance. An even more complex plan might anticipate the interaction of separate initiatives—for example, pairing increased funding with a system of rewards for schools that improve and penalties for schools that fail.

We distinguish a simple reform plan from a more completely thought-out strategy along the lines laid out in *Fixing Urban Schools*. A citywide strategy is an integrated approach to incentives for school performance, investments in school capabilities, and freedom for schools to change. Figure 4-1 illustrates the combination of incentives, investments, and freedom of action.

A set of actions lacking even one of these three elements is not a logically complete strategy for school improvement. Similarly, a strategy in which one element is poorly developed or ill matched with the others is a weak one. A reform plan whose elements are not designed to complement one another, do not all affect the same schools, or are not timed to act simultaneously is not truly a strategy.[1]

Strategy implies intention. A locality that increases spending on some schools and creates a system of rewards and penalties for other schools will have two unrelated initiatives, not one strategy. Similarly, a locality that creates mixed signals for schools, declaring on one hand a plan to apply rewards and penalties for school performance but on the other hand offering assurances that every employee's job, salary, and work assignment are secure would not have a strategy.

Many of the cities had unrelated initiatives that did not combine to work together on all schools. For example, Boston has a small group of within-district charter schools (pilot schools) that enjoy considerable freedom of action and have stronger incentives to demonstrate perfor-

Figure 4-1. *Elements of Reform Strategy*

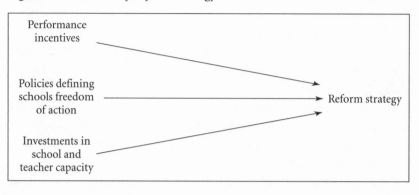

mance and retain parents' confidence than other schools. Pilot schools were not included in the summary of Boston's initiative in chapter 2 because the superintendent and allied community leaders consider them irrelevant, not part of their reform strategy. Chartering might strengthen Boston's strategy, in which performance incentives and school freedom of action are not well developed. But because it applies to only a few isolated schools, we do not consider chartering part of the city's strategy.

In other cities, major investments were made in the capabilities of a few notable schools, but these were idiosyncratic events, not the result of a coordinated districtwide strategy. Similarly, some cities had a few schools that had great freedom of action, but this was a result of historical events or special arrangements and had no impact on other schools; these arrangements are by definition not part of the city's strategy.

Building Blocks

Our ideas about new strategies come from several sources: reform strategies employed in other countries and in fields other than education, the alternative theories of education reform we studied in *Fixing Urban Schools*, and our simulations. From these sources it is clear that potentially much stronger and more promising strategies can be created to reform city schools. These strategies would create stronger incentives for school performance, require more investment in school and teacher

Table 4-1. *Education Reform Designs Combining Different Cities' Strengths*

School performance incentives	Capabilities investments	School freedom of action
New York City District 2's practice of transferring uncooperative staff to other NYC community districts	Memphis and San Antonio's use of New American Schools design teams	Seattle's school control of funds and teacher hiring
San Antonio and San Francisco's reconstitution threat	New York City District 2's use of carefully picked advice and assistance	San Francisco's allowing troubled schools to spend desegregation funds into struggling schools
New York City District 2's school-specific performance agreements	Boston's use of school improvement teams	New York City District 2's allowing principals total freedom of action within their superintendent-approved improvement plans
Seattle and New York City District 2's use of limited parent choice		

capacity, and provide for greater school freedom of action than those that have been employed in any city's education reform strategy.

This analysis serves as background for a more important task, which is to create combined strategies that would be stronger than any one city's reform initiative. What if the strongest parts of different cities' reform designs were combined so that elements of wishful thinking in one district were replaced by design elements that created strong school performance incentives, investments in school capabilities, and real school freedom of action? Table 4-1 identifies some reform elements from the six cities that promise to address the tripartite need for incentives, investment, and deregulation. Different combinations of these could become the basis of promising new strategies.

Three very promising reform strategies could be assembled from the parts of table 4-1. First, a city could create very strong performance incentives by combining school-specific performance agreements, the threat of reconstituting failed schools, and parent choice. In effect, schools that could not fulfill their performance agreements with the superintendent and could not avoid having large numbers of parents petition to transfer their children to schools elsewhere would be subject to reconstitution.

These performance incentives could be coupled with serious investments in teacher and school capability, for example in the form of district- and philanthropy-funded school improvement teams assembled, as in Boston, from the best talent available in area universities, school districts, and nonprofit organizations. These arrangements could be further coupled with policies defining greater freedom of action for schools, such as assurances that school staffs could choose new teachers and even petition to remove able but uncooperative teachers from their buildings.

A second promising reform strategy from table 4-1 might combine a reconstitution threat with district help to schools wishing to work with New American Schools design teams or other independent assistance providers, plus a transfer of significant amounts of new money for schools to spend any ways their leaders thought might improve student performance.

A third strategy would combine Seattle's limited parent-choice plan (in which families can choose schools outside their neighborhoods as long as transfers do not worsen racial imbalances), help from any assistance provider a school prefers, and the superintendent's help in finding new money for schools according to an improvement plan initiated by the principal and approved by the superintendent.

These are not the only ways of creating combined reform strategies, and leaders in every community will face their own combinations of needs, political constraints, and opportunities. But any possible combined strategy should be assessed on the criteria of how well it promotes school incentives, capabilities, and freedom of action.

Not every potential combined strategy is a good one. City leaders are often tempted to create strategies that involve new financial investments but avoid strong school performance incentives. Many local reform strategies include talk about increased school freedom of action but never make clear what schools will have the freedom to do and what the school board and central office must stop doing.[2]

It would be feasible to create the worst of all possible worlds by pooling cities' subjects of wishful thinking. For example, combining Boston's lack of performance incentives with Seattle's lack of a professional development strategy and San Francisco's limitations on school freedom of action (maintained in the name of peace between the central office and the teachers' union) would guarantee stagnation. A slightly stronger, but still implausible, hybrid might combine Seattle's reliance on weak parent-choice provisions as its main performance incentive, San Francisco's effort to reconstitute failed schools without giving principals and lead teachers time to devise curriculum and build a like-minded staff, and San Antonio's reduction of schools' freedom of action by imposing a new teacher training initiative every year.

School Performance Incentives

There are many ways to create strong incentives for school performance. These incentives can be both negative, creating powerful consequences for schools that will not or cannot improve, and positive, creating opportunities for recognition and professional advancement of teachers and principals who succeed in challenging situations. They include the following.

—Giving families open choice among public schools. The need to attract families and build loyalties gives teachers and principals strong incentives to clarify the school's goals and methods so parents have a basis for choice, work closely with individual children, collaborate with one another, and demonstrate performance.

—Promoting competition among schools. A city policy of creating new schools or encouraging charter schools to form in neighborhoods with weak schools makes it clear that teachers and principals are in the same boat and must make the best possible use of their pooled time and talent. Permitting low-income students from failing schools to transfer to private schools also creates performance incentives for public school staff.

—Creating professional and earnings opportunities for high-performing teachers and principals. Initiatives allowing teachers and principals in high-performing schools to expand their schools or open branches in new neighborhoods, or permitting staff members from successful schools to charge for help and advice given to other schools, creates both group and individual performance incentives.

—Allowing individual teachers and principals to negotiate salary and work assignments with schools. A teacher labor market gives every teacher a strong reason to build a reputation by making valuable contributions to his or her school. It also allows professionals with excellent reputa-

tions to negotiate high pay and interesting assignments regardless of how old they are or how many degrees they hold. (This arrangement also creates freedom of action for schools.)

All of these proposals are, to say the least, controversial. They are, however, both more promising and less dangerous than stakeholders in the existing public education system would allege.[3]

Investments in School Capacity

Investments in school capacity can also be promoted in various ways. Some involve segmenting funds so that investments are made, and others involve creating new sources of assistance for schools.

—*Guaranteeing every school a minimum set-aside* for purchasing materials, advice, and assistance. This guarantees that no school will be unable to work on improving its instructional program. It also prevents school staff from eating their seed corn by spending every cent on current services and investing nothing in new capabilities.

—*Creating independent new institutions* to provide assistance, advice, and teacher training. This can increase the options available to schools and make them less dependent on whatever the central office bureaucracy can offer. It can also make the central office professional development providers more customer friendly.

—*Setting up "venture capital" funds to encourage formation of new nonprofit and university-based assistance organizations.* This can create an entrepreneurial sector that is constantly searching for ways to help individual schools. Coupled with a good privately funded users' guide to sources of assistance, it can also increase the options available to schools.

—*Creating a new-schools incubator.* Incubators for schools, like business incubators, can help ensure that teachers and principals charged with opening a new school are fully prepared for the instructional and managerial challenges they must face. It can also generate the capacity to create new schools to compete with failing ones, which is necessary for some of the school performance incentives already discussed.

These options are less controversial than the ones listed under "incentives." They are, however, expensive. All of them imply changes in public spending and long-term business and foundation investment.

Arrangements for School Freedom of Action

Guaranteeing that school communities—administrators, teachers, staff, and parents—have the freedom to change their schools in ways that might work better for students may not be as difficult as many imagine. Consider the following.

—*Supervising schools via performance agreements,* not codes of rules. This allows school staffs to focus on one problem only, how to improve instruction and student learning, and can at least in theory eliminate public schools' unproductive preoccupation with compliance.

—*Giving schools real-dollar budgets and the discretion to spend money.* This, more than anything else, makes it clear that schools are in control of their instructional programs and are responsible for choices about materials, assistance, and teacher training.

—*Assuring schools that they can reallocate and spend the money they save by reducing expenditures.* This ensures that schools can gain something by identifying things they no longer need to do or buy and increases the likelihood that school leaders will carefully review expenditures in light of needs. In the past, many schools have been reluctant to cut unnecessary expenditures because they expected that some other entity—the school board, central office, or state treasurer—would capture the benefits.

—*Allowing schools to decide how they will organize and staff themselves.* This ensures that schools can optimize their staffing for instruction. Judging from the experience of independent and charter schools, it is likely to simplify administrative structures and increase the amount of time adults spend in contact with students.

—*Allowing schools to choose whom to hire and, within wide boundaries, what to pay them.* This allows schools to choose and reward people according to their fit with the school's program and to seek a productive mix of highly paid senior and less expensive junior teachers. It also allows schools to pay high salaries to people they consider indispensable and to keep good teachers and principals who might, under a district-controlled personnel system, be bumped by more senior people or transferred involuntarily. (This arrangement also improves performance incentives by letting schools define and keep the coherent programs necessary to compete for students and by encouraging teachers to build their reputations as productive team members).

These options require significant changes in the ways public school systems do business. Public school teachers and administrators who have accommodated themselves to bureaucratic and civil service environments will find these ideas unfamiliar and threatening. They do not, however, require competencies beyond the reach of intelligent and well-educated people: people in small businesses, nonprofit organizations, and private and independent schools function in such an environment all the time. A city choosing such approaches to school freedom of action will, however, need to make corresponding investments in training, organizational incubation, and recruitment of people who can lead schools and teach under conditions that demand performance.

New Strategies

Taken together, these new ideas introduce three features that are either missing or barely evident in today's public education: choice, competition, and entrepreneurship. Every one of the building blocks we have described is guaranteed to perturb someone—school board members, central office administrators, people who fear marketlike mechanisms, or teachers who value civil service protection over opportunities for innovation and advancement. None of the ideas is magic by itself, and every one of them can be implemented badly. However, if assembled into well-balanced strategies, these ideas about performance incentives, capacity investment, and school freedom of action can compensate for one another's weaknesses and create new hopes for urban school performance. This section formulates some of the most promising new strategies.

Table 4-2 summarizes three of these strategies. In the first a CEO-style superintendent manages a portfolio of strong, distinctive schools. In the second a superintendent and school board create a diverse system of public schools by entering into performance contracts with independent organizations: groups of teachers and parents, teacher cooperatives and unions, nonprofit human service organizations, colleges and universities, civic groups, and for-profit contractors. The third option attempts to make the educational resources of an entire urban community

Table 4-2. *Three New Education Reform Strategies*

Strategy	Incentives	Capabilities investments	School freedom of action
CEO–strong schools	Superintendent uses state standards as the basis of yearly agreements on each school's strategy and performance; can reassign staff, open and close schools	Funds are set aside for investment in new methods, materials, and teacher training. Superintendent helps schools find the best providers of help	Schools control improvement funds as long as they fulfill agreements with superintendent. School staffs can initiate staff transfers and choose new hires
Diverse providers	Every school works under a contract that specifies instructional approach and goals for students. Parents can choose schools. New contracts are established to replace failing schools	District recruits and stimulates many independent sources of curricular advice, instructional materials, and teacher training. Schools choose the ones that meet their needs	Schools control all funds, hire staff, and purchase their own advisors and providers of assistance. Teachers may unionize at the school level
Community partnerships	One public coordinating board stimulates supply of schools, allocates funds on a per pupil basis to any school a child attends, licenses public and private groups variously to operate and charter schools. Parents choose schools	Campaign for private investment creates resources for strapped independent schools, encourages nonschool community and cultural resources to pitch in, and brokers public and private resources for social and other services	Money comes to schools on a per pupil basis. Schools control all funds, hire staff, and purchase their own advisors and providers of assistance. Teachers may unionize at the school level

available for the education of the city's children. These strategies create new combinations of strong incentives, serious investments in school capabilities, and real freedom of action to allow schools to solve problems.[4] Except in states that allow districts to become all charter and let charter school leaders control real-dollar budgets and staffing decisions, none of these strategies is possible under current laws and regulations. Chapter 6 identifies some crucial state legislative and regulatory changes that city leaders might lobby for in support of their reform strategies.

The CEO–Strong Schools Strategy

Under the CEO strategy the local superintendent would operate as the head of a decentralized enterprise. As the chief executive officer he or she would know that the real work is done at the school level. The superintendent's job would be to ensure that teachers and principals have every possible performance incentive, source of help, and freedom of action they need to serve students well. The superintendent would make sure nothing inhibits school productivity. Although the superintendent would have the authority to make rules or require schools to hire particular people or use the services of the school system central office, the only reason he or she would impose such constraints would be to improve school productivity.

The most important transactions between a CEO-superintendent and an individual school would occur with reference to the school's annual performance agreement. This agreement, negotiated between school leadership and the CEO, would identify each school's instructional deficiencies and define plans to improve instruction. It would also provide grants of authority to the school to spend money and train, hire, and fire staff in fulfillment of its instructional improvement plan. The CEO could also require, as a condition of approval of a school's plan, replacement of teachers and principals who had not acted as promised under previous school plans.

The superintendent would also commit to helping schools find appropriate sources of assistance. School freedom of action would be guaranteed by the CEO's express approval of staffing, scheduling, and other changes consistent with the school improvement plan. The CEO would have the authority to designate another group to take over or compete with a school that could not formulate or would not execute a plausible improvement plan. This would guarantee freedom of action and also protect children from being trapped in stagnant, low-performing schools.

The CEO–Strong Schools strategy is a fully realized version of what Anthony Alvarado attempted in New York City District 2. It also draws on the experience of two other superintendent-led cities, Chicago and Charlotte, N.C.[5] But it is stronger than those cities' reform initiatives. The superintendent unequivocally has the power to close or overhaul schools that do not follow through on their performance agreements and can open new schools to replace or compete with mediocre schools. When their school performance agreements permit it, principals have the unequivocal power to define teacher jobs and hiring criteria and (subject to the laws protecting all American workers) select and terminate staff.[6]

The CEO–Strong Schools strategy is very different from other systems in which superintendents have been prominent but have not rigorously implemented performance agreements with schools. In John Stanford's Seattle initiative, for example, the superintendent exercised extraordinary personal influence and freedom of unilateral action, but whenever he was not able to attend to a problem personally, it was managed through traditional bureaucratic processes. Even when Stanford was personally engaged, school principals could not assume that the central office bureaucracy would respect agreements they made with the superintendent. Moreover, because none of Stanford's practices was stabilized by permanent changes in the roles and missions of the school board, central office, teachers' union, or principals, his successor does not have the freedom of action Stanford had. The CEO–Strong Schools strategy is also very different from the reform initiative in Philadelphia, where superintendent David Hornbeck is trying to promote innovation and initiative without decentralizing control of staffing or funds or creating school-specific performance agreements.

The Diverse Providers Strategy

The Diverse Providers strategy is a widely recognized option that has not been seriously tried by any American city. We only sketch it here; many thorough analyses of this proposal are available.[7]

Under this strategy the local school board would aggressively use the power delegated to it by the state to provide public schools. It could maintain some publicly managed schools but would also use contracts to support public schools run by independent providers. All schools, whether managed by the traditional school system or by independent contractors, would have similar performance agreements and freedom of action. The school board could not be more lenient with schools run by the traditional public school system nor could it impose more constraints on those schools than on independent contractors. Conversely, the board could not be more lenient with independent contractors or impose requirements on them that schools overseen and managed by the district were not also required to meet.

Schools would receive real-dollar funding on a per pupil basis and spend money at their own discretion, bounded only by their contractual commitments. School boards could hold back only small amounts of funds to support their oversight of individual schools. Thus schools would control almost all public funds and would make their own investments and purchase advice and assistance. To prevent unwarranted subsidies to wealthy families, schools that accepted public funds would not be allowed to charge extra tuition.

Schools would admit students via a publicly managed lottery in which every student who applied had an equal chance of acceptance. No student could be excluded, although schools could tell parents in advance what levels of student attendance, effort, and deportment are required. Schools would choose and pay for their own instructional methods, staffing patterns, and sources of help. They would also employ teachers and negotiate pay, benefits, and responsibilities.

The school board would be able—even obligated—to shift contracts from poorly performing school providers to more promising ones. The board would therefore have a strong incentive to encourage promising new providers. Parents would have choices among all publicly funded schools.

An analog to the Diverse Providers strategy can be found in the United States in higher education. Many states oversee higher education with coordinating boards of various kinds in just this way. For example, Washington State's Higher Education Coordinating Board considers the demand for higher education and directs state investment to subject matters and geographic areas that are not well served by existing institutions. It considers what is available from community colleges and privately operated universities (including some for-profit schools) as well as from state-run colleges and universities. It also makes available forms of state aid that students can use at private colleges. State-operated institutions are well represented on that board, but so are other providers and user groups.

At the K–12 level, however, there are few if any real-world examples of the Diverse Providers strategy. Small districts in Colorado, California, and Georgia are attempting to establish charters for all their schools. Chicago is experimenting with forms of contracting, as are Portland, Oregon, and Wichita, Kansas. A proposed Pennsylvania state law would permit contracting for most or all Philadelphia schools under some circumstances. However, it is not clear whether these districts will allow anyone other than their own employees to propose and operate charters nor whether the charters will be real contracts between independent parties or simply agreements that the school board can amend unilaterally at any time.

The Diverse Providers strategy implies that individual schools will be regulated only through their contracts and will operate as independent enterprises. As the research team of the Center on Reinventing Public Education has learned in an ongoing study of charter schools' relationship with government, few agreements between charter operators and their government sponsors are so clear or give schools such freedom of action. Thus despite the fact that the Diverse Providers strategy is based on now familiar ideas, it probably does not exist anywhere.

In providing for contracts for new schools, the Diverse Providers strategy only requires the school board to set minimum requirements to protect children and parents from incompetent providers. Judging from current practices in private school licensing, licensing requirements would not be extensive. Licenses would require that schools be held accountable for performance under state student performance standards and would sustain public sector guarantees of fair admission, civil rights protection, health, and safety.

Licenses would provide the same basic protections now offered by state approval of private schools: they would say that a school is of sufficient quality that parents can send their children there confident that the school meets minimum state requirements. States and localities now apparently assume that children in private schools require only a few basic protections about subjects to be taught and the presence of at least some highly qualified teachers and administrators. The fact that state codes pertaining to public schools are orders of magnitude longer and more detailed is apparently due to states' need to ensure probity in the use of public funds, satisfy federal auditors, encode agreements made with the school construction industry, and protect the collective bargaining rights of public employees.

An Even Bolder Option

An even more original approach is possible. The Community Partnerships strategy is based on a radical approach to improving educational opportunities in a city. It acknowledges that the traditional boundaries between the public school system's responsibilities and those of other community agencies are themselves part of the educational problem. As one of this idea's originators, Lawrence Pierce, has contended, what we refer to as the Community Partnerships strategy opens new options for education, asking "How can this community use all its assets to provide the best education for all our children?" Of the three options outlined in this book, this strategy best defines the concept that "it takes a city."

The Community Partnership strategy can be seen as a further development of the Diverse Providers approach. Under Diverse Providers a family would be free to choose any school for its children. Perhaps more important, Diverse Providers defines government's responsibility to ensure that a wide range of options is accessible to children in every area of the city. It also blurs the line between public and private: any school that improves the range of high-quality options available and meets other licensing requirements (accountability under state standards, race- and income-blind admissions) could be licensed to receive public per pupil funding. Families that chose to send children to schools that would not accept the public per pupil subsidy as full tuition would have to pay the full cost themselves.

The Community Partnerships strategy would also include multiple public and private providers.[8] It would in addition be a genuine communitywide system in that all the community's resources, not simply its schools, would be available in an organized way to meet children's educational needs and their general well-being. A new community authority would oversee the supply of educational opportunities for all children. It would license many entities to provide K–12 instruction, including conventional public school systems, contractors of the kind described under the Diverse Providers strategy, unconventional educational and cultural options, including museums, libraries, arts agencies, church-supported systems, willing to operate under First Amendment constraints, and dispersed "cyber schools." The only educational institutions excluded would be those that could not be licensed, refused to be considered part of a public system, or would not accept the public per pupil expenditure as full payment of tuition. As in the Diverse Providers strategy, parents would have choices among all these educational forms.

Community Partnerships would go beyond Diverse Providers in three ways. In addition to contracting for publicly funded schools, a community education board would do the following.

ENCOURAGE NONSCHOOL EDUCATIONAL RESOURCES. The board would encourage other educational and cultural institutions to strengthen and supplement school instructional offerings, paying particular attention to community enclaves with large numbers of disadvantaged children. Thus it would encourage museums and libraries to supplement arts and history instruction in schools serving low-income neighborhoods. It might even encourage the formation of teacher cooperatives that could contract to offer in-school instruction in areas where particular schools were weak: for example, a cooperative for scientists and engineers could offer science and mathematics instruction in middle and high schools lacking qualified teachers. The idea here is that city leaders should set out confidently to provide to children of the poor the same kinds of superior out-of-school learning opportunities that are routinely made available to children of affluence through access to magazines and reading materials in the home and family trips and outings of various kinds.

PRESERVE A PORTFOLIO OF EDUCATIONAL ALTERNATIVES FOR THE DISADVANTAGED. Any fair-sized city enjoys a variety of educational and cultural resources serving disadvantaged children, many of the entities independent and nonprofit. Some are schools; many are not.

Most of these entities are financially marginal, living hand-to-mouth and dependent on securing one small grant after another so they can provide services such as music lessons or a summer camp experience to poor students, often inexpensively or free. These invisible community-based institutions are vital to urban well-being, and in the interests of community the board should campaign for private donations to help strengthen and preserve them. This assistance should also be extended to financially troubled private schools, including those affiliated with specific churches and religions, if they can demonstrate a history of dedication to meeting the needs of disadvantaged students. Finally, the board could think about creating ways of providing assistance in the form of curriculum, guidance, and other resources for home schoolers. In preserving a portfolio of educational alternatives for the disadvantaged, the board should adopt the attitude that there is no such thing as too many educational options.

BROKER HEALTH AND SOCIAL SERVICE RESOURCES TO MEET CHILDREN'S NEEDS. It is probably an exaggeration to say that schools traditionally have ignored the out-of-school health, mental health, and social services needs of children and their families. But it is no exaggeration to say that most educators believe that if children are not learning because they do not receive community services, that is somebody else's problem.

To be sure, schools cannot solve these problems. Nonetheless, city leaders intent on improving school performance have to mobilize out-of-school expertise and resources to tackle these challenges. Thus, the community board should act as a broker for a wide variety of preschool, school readiness, health, mental health, and family social services for children in need, provided either in schools or in collaboratives working closely with schools. The board should ensure that resources go where they are most needed (not just where they are easiest to provide or to some parents and staff that have the best access to service providers). It should work to make sure that schools get the services considered to be the highest priority, not simply what they had to accept; and it should worry about accountability, insisting that public and private agencies participating in the effort measure their performance by services provided to children and families and results observed, not the number of planning committees organized and meetings attended.

The Shape and Nature of the Community Education Board

The community education board would have broader functions under Community Partnerships strategy than under Diverse Providers. It should therefore be more broadly representative, including some elected or mayorally appointed public members, and some ex officio representatives of such community institutions as the United Way, major private charities, foundations dedicated to education and cultural affairs, public libraries and museums, independent schools, and faith-based and community-based organizations.

In performing the three functions we have outlined, the board needs to influence the actions of independent organizations. If it is to be effective, it should set out to persuade public and private agencies to create new services needed by particular schools. If it is to do its job well, it should control as much of the community's public funds as possible. That is to say, it should control all public school funds and, if possible, all local public social service monies in programs focused on children. Foundations and businesses could strengthen the board by donating funds to it rather than to particular projects. In the ideal situation, under the Community Partnership model the board would allocate all public social and health service resources on a real-dollar basis, as it would public funds for formal instruction.

This community education board would control all funds for public education and would write checks to schools based on their enrollments. It could enter master contracts with local public systems, but it would also be free to license other providers to serve children in the same areas. Public school boards would receive per pupil amounts for all children served by their school, but nothing extra. Public school boards could then run their own schools or contract with independent providers for them. Because their schools would compete with other schools run under very different auspices, public school boards would have strong incentives to eliminate unnecessary overhead costs and put as much money into the schools (and instruction) as possible.

The community board should also hold back a small amount of money to incubate new schools and encourage development of new options for poorly served groups or neighborhoods. Public school boards, with their portfolios of schools and economies of scale, would presumably have an advantage over smaller providers when it came to meeting new needs.

No localities have chosen a reform strategy as bold as this. Like Diverse Providers it encourages a public capacity to oversee and license schools and stimulate formation of new schools to meet emerging community needs. But it goes well beyond Diverse Providers by establishing a unique opportunity for integration of public education with other community assets, including human services. The community board could control public human services funds, allocate them according to locally developed priorities, and license organizations to receive them on the basis of appropriateness and quality of services. It could also provide a forum for the voluntary coordination of privately funded and foundation-funded human services.

If state law allowed such a board to control all funds now going to publicly supported human service organizations, it could charter new organizations that would provide both schooling and social services for a defined group of children. Such comprehensive child development organizations would operate more like public service, civic, and faith-based charitable groups than school bureaucracies, offering families that chose them a range of learning and support opportunities, all built around a school or integrated with school offerings.

Choosing a Reform Strategy

None of the three reform strategies might be right for any particular city. Cities will inevitably choose strategies that suit their unique histories and political environments. Urban school systems that undergo mayoral takeover are also likely to choose strategies that accord with the mayor's philosophy of government and political commitments.

In general, however, it is a grave mistake for a city undergoing some form of school takeover by a mayor or group of leading citizens to choose a strategy because it is the one most like those the leaders are familiar with or the one with which the greatest number of stakeholders in the current system are comfortable. (See *Fixing Urban Schools*, chapter 5, for an extended discussion of why reproducing the conventional system strategy is also the surest way to continue current levels of school performance.) In choosing a reform strategy it is important for city leaders to expressly consider alternatives and face facts about what is gained and lost by rejecting bolder strategies such as those we have described. The losses will be felt in results that are slower to come, in part because the reforms are unlikely to establish strong incentives for performance and clear freedom of action for schools.

Table 4-3 analyzes circumstances that might predispose a city toward one or another reform strategy. It indicates that what a city determined to improve its schools does should depend to a great extent on the crisis it faces. The CEO–Strong Schools strategy is probably the least appropriate for a city whose school system has deteriorated far enough to require a takeover. This strategy needs enough political stability to sustain an aggressive superintendent in office for a long time, an excellent teaching force, principals who can respond quickly to new opportunities and incentives, and a tradition of good public sector management. Almost by definition, a school system under threat of takeover possesses none of these strengths.

The Diverse Providers strategy, however, fits many big cities, especially those with capable colleges, universities, nonprofit organizations, cultural institutions, and community groups. In fact, because it sidesteps, by design, many of the weaknesses of the existing system, it might prove to be the most effective reform of all for many urban areas.

The Community Partnerships strategy requires many of the same circumstances as Diverse Providers plus a strong philanthropic community to help build a broad supply of school providers and a strong infrastructure of school-assistance organizations and human services. The Community Partnerships strategy is the most likely to upset stakeholders in the current public education system and, because it takes on a comprehensive human services mission as well, it will also upset welfare and training bureaucracies. But its aggressive use of all community education resources merits a look from culturally rich cities with weak public school systems, such as Chicago, Philadelphia, Detroit, Los Angeles, and St. Louis.

Some readers, unfortunately, may find their cities fit the Diverse Providers and the Community Partnership options in both the first and

Table 4-3. *Appropriate and Inappropriate Circumstances for the Education Reform Strategies*

Strategy	Appropriate	Inappropriate
CEO–strong schools	Tradition of strong superintendent leadership, high-quality teachers in many schools, able principals, and a tradition of probity in public sector funds management	Unstable superintendency, weak teaching force, history of misuse of funds by school leaders, presence of many strong educational institutions outside the public school system
Diverse providers	Many weak public schools, lack of a strong principal corps, presence of many cultural institutions willing to operate schools	Only a few weak public schools, strong principal leadership corps, few educational or cultural institutions capable of or interested in operating schools
Community partnerships	Many weak public schools, weak system and school leadership, business and foundations capable of making major investments in new school creation, strong infrastructure of other educational and cultural institutions, and a variety of faith- and community-based service organizations	Strong public dislike for market solutions, absolute state constitutional barriers to church-provided public instruction, weak infrastructure of other cultural and educational institutions, and few faith- or community-based service organizations

second columns of table 4-3. These cities suffer from a mismatch between their education reform needs and their local institutional and political realities. Unfortunately, there is no easy answer for a city in this situation. Most cities, even those whose schools have failed to the extent that courts, legislatures, or mayors have felt compelled to assume control, have shied away from strong actions that might be effective. Cleveland's school system has been taken over twice because politics as usual quickly brought the system back to the same place it had started.

Baltimore and Washington, D.C., might also need a second takeover, and though the politically moderate and nonconfrontational Boston strategy reported here is alive and well, slow progress could lead to new takeover pressures.

Tragically, cities where no one is able to devote a great deal of political capital, skill, and determination to school reform are not likely to choose reforms strong enough to work. They are likely to continue to experience a series of palatable but ultimately unproductive reform initiatives.

Administrative Arrangements

Most new reform efforts pay very little attention to the administrative infrastructure required to keep changes on track. Mayors and leaders interested in institutionalizing reform cannot afford this mistake.

The three reform strategies proposed in this chapter are strong on performance incentives, provide mechanisms for investment in school capacities, and provide for enough freedom of action so that schools can take responsibility for their own instructional improvement. By design they overcome many of the factors that, according to political scientists, make it difficult for teachers to teach, schools to focus on instruction, and school boards to create and stick with coherent policies.[9] Frederick Hess, for example, identifies two obstacles to public education reform: policy churn caused by the constant enactment of new measures, and political isolation caused by the bureaucratic and professional domination of issues that affect the whole community.[10] The senior author of this book, writing elsewhere, has identified a closely related but finer-grained set of obstacles.[11]

—Initiatives that weaken schools by adding new programs and mandates.

—Misconceptions about democracy that compel elected officials to search for the one districtwide policy or investment that will lead to universal school improvement.

—Episodic crisis intervention from civic and political leaders who seize on plausible but logically incomplete initiatives and then pass on to other matters, only to return when the last solution proves unsuccessful.

—School system leadership instability, especially the rapid turnover of superintendents, leading to frequent and abrupt changes of improvement strategy and equally abrupt abandonment of half-accomplished reforms.

The three strategies we have outlined are designed to deal with these obstacles. They eliminate school boards' ability to impose new mandates and focus board efforts on creating incentives, capacity investments, and the freedom needed by a system of strong schools. They eliminate school boards' power of the purse by ensuring that money flows to schools on a basis of student population. They put schools, not elected officials or central office bureaucrats, in charge of the search for methods and programs that work for the specific children they serve. By decentralizing teacher hiring and pay decisions, they eliminate the ability of school boards (and teachers' unions) to control schools by dictating whom they will employ. Finally, these strategies reduce the significance (and therefore the causes) of superintendent turnover by making reform strategy a lasting civic commitment buttressed by private investment and mayoral support, not simply an attractive agenda relying on the initiative and prestige of one individual.

But none of the strategies is self-executing. Each assumes that someone will take responsibility for activities that are now either neglected or not performed at all. At present, few cities have institutions capable of implementing any of the new strategies.

Except in New York City District 2, there is no person or group prepared to negotiate performance agreements with individual schools and enforce them in practice. No city has a school board or community oversight board that can manage a portfolio of contracts with diverse school providers. None has shown the ability to close schools that persistently perform poorly. None has developed an institutionalized capability to incubate competent new teams of teachers and administrators who can take over failing schools or compete with them. None has a mechanism for creating and overseeing universal parent choice, ensuring that schools have access to the most capable teachers available in the metropolitan area, or allocating funds directly to schools. None knows how to run a parent choice system that cannot be manipulated by aggressive families or does not exacerbate class and race segregation. Few of the cities have broken the central office monopoly on advice to schools, school performance assessment, and teacher evaluation; and none has developed good alternative providers for these functions.

Thus the new strategy options have their own zones of wishful thinking. These are weaknesses not of basic strategy but of institutional roles, missions, and capacity. The next chapter shows how city leaders prepared to create a powerful reform strategy can also create the institutions required to bring it into being and realize its full potential.

Holding a Strategy in Place 5

H OW CAN MAYORS, community leaders, the school system, city government, higher education institutions, business, and philanthropic
and faith-based groups divide labor to make education reform strategies work? Putting into operation any of the reform strategies suggested
in chapter 4 will require hard work and serious investment. Without clear
assignments of responsibility, any strategy will fail.

What we are talking about here is changing the structure and mission
of the local school system so that it smoothly executes the reform strategy instead of fighting it or treating it as a foreign body.

Many of the reform initiatives examined in chapters 2, 3, and 4 might
have survived even a school board spasm or a superintendent's departure if the supporting structures had been in place. But most initiatives
focus on the school system structure, neglecting the difficult work required to create the needed institutional capabilities to ensure the reform's
success and leaving in place organizational structures and inclinations
dedicated to things inconsistent with the reform strategy.

This chapter is about organizing for the long-term implementation,
refinement, and renewal of the initial reform strategy. It argues that we
need to eliminate some institutions, change the missions and capabili-

ties of others, and create new institutions. Some of the most important new institutional capabilities should exist outside what we now consider the central office.

Institutional arrangements for school reform require a division of labor among people who (among many other things) teach; manage schools; set policy; hire principals and teachers; allocate dollars, staff, and other resources to schools; raise money; purchase and maintain school buildings; establish learning goals and student performance standards; and assess the effectiveness of schools and the system as a whole. Institutional arrangements can be well matched with a reform design. Leaders can make sure that responsibilities for crucial actions are clearly assigned and that the people with the responsibility have the power to do what is required. Institutional arrangements can also, obviously, be poorly matched to the reform design. Responsibility for key items on the agenda may be unclear or everyone may consider their responsibilities under the reform design secondary to other interests or obligations.

The first step toward establishing institutional arrangements for each of the reform strategies described in chapter 4 is to enumerate the functions that must be performed if the particular strategy is to succeed. The analysis of zones of wishful thinking is an important part of that effort. To our knowledge, no big city (or other community of any size) has fully institutionalized the following four functions, each required no matter which of the three reform strategies is adopted:

—managing a diverse portfolio of educational options for all the city's children;

—helping every school, whatever its clientele or approach to instruction, perform its mission well;

—monitoring and reporting on the effectiveness of all community educational options so that parents can understand their choices and the community can evaluate system results; and

—making sure that schools have access to the best possible choices of teachers, materials, and equipment.

Some cities have good public school bureaucracies, but none of them would equate their mission with these four functions. Currently, by law and custom, the mission of a school system bureaucracy is to apply policies made by legislatures and school boards, not to nurture a diverse supply of schools. Every city's school bureaucracy defines public education as the schools and instructional programs it directly operates, controls, and funds; none considers either independent schools or other community educational assets to be part of public education.

All public school bureaucracies supply schools, but few think it is their job to reproduce popular schools that are overenrolled until the demand is satisfied. Few bureaucracies take responsibility for providing good value-added assessments of school effectiveness, and none can precisely track the flow of dollars to schools and students. All hire teachers, but few aggressively seek the best teachers in the country or consider seriously whether recruiting new teachers from an entirely different pool would do more to improve the teaching force than would more in-service training of incumbent teachers.

Box 5-1 provides a more detailed list of the institutional functions required by the reform strategies suggested in chapter 3. This list comes from our own analysis, buttressed by others' earlier work. Anthony Bryk and colleagues have conducted a detailed analysis of extraschool functions that must be performed in order for Chicago's reform strategy to have all the hoped-for effects on schools (a mixture of our CEO–Strong Schools and Diverse Providers strategies).[1] Their analysis of functions nicely parallels Anthony Bryk and Paul Hill's review of six decentralizing school systems, an earlier Chicago analysis of support structures in a reformed school system, Donald McAdams's review of Houston's emerging school reform strategy, David Kearns and James Harvey's analysis of the requirements of a higher-performing school system, and Chester Finn, Gregg Vanourek, and Bruno Manno's analysis of requirements for a system of charter schools.[2]

The three new reform strategies introduced in chapter 4 place great emphasis on conscious management of a portfolio of schools, assuming that the size, location, staffing, instructional methods, and in some cases the division of labor between private and public participants in the management of schools will change from time to time. The CEO–Strong Schools strategy makes the superintendent a portfolio manager but assumes that most schools will be operated by public employees.[3]

The Diverse Providers strategy assumes that the school board will be the portfolio manager and that it will choose different mixes of school providers at different times, some public, some independent nonprofit, and possibly even some for-profit. In addition to encouraging attention

Box 5-1. *Functions Requiring New Institutional Arrangements No Matter Which Strategy Is Employed*

Portfolio management: determining the mix of educational options for the city's children
—Authorizing schools to receive public funds (and determining that some schools will no longer be supported)
—Making sure that the best use is being made of all community education assets, including libraries, other schools, and so on
—Determining whether the current mix of schools meets important community needs (or whether some groups are poorly served by current schools and need a school or program that is not now available)
—Incubating new schools: ensuring that principals and teachers assigned to open new schools or take over failed schools that are being reconstituted have opportunities to plan their instructional program, prepare to perform necessary budgeting and administrative tasks, and recruit teachers and students

Fostering school development: helping every school perform its mission well
—Buffering schools from state and federal regulations that militate against effective instruction*
—Making sure schools have adequate and equal resources (or that differences in resources reflect policy, not administrative aberrations)
—Training school leaders and local site council leaders
—Providing school-level organizational development
—Fostering creation of networks of like-minded schools

to out-of-school needs, the Community Partnership option assumes that public bodies will license schools, but that they will do so liberally and that the supply of schools will reflect the initiative of nonprofit groups, teacher-led cooperatives and enterprises, civic and cultural organizations, postsecondary education institutions, profit-seeking entrepreneurs, and faith-based and community-based groups.

Each of the new strategies forces significant changes in the ways the public school system operates. Currently, the superintendent and the bureaucracy (acting on behalf of the school board) are formally respon-

System performance: monitoring and reporting on school effectiveness
—Maintaining and analyzing data to ensure proper fiscal management
—Analyzing and reporting on the productivity of individual schools and the system as a whole
—Sponsoring inspections and quality reviews on school resources and programs to assess whether schools are implementing their improvement plans

Making sure schools get the best available teachers, equipment, and materials
—Ensuring that schools receive, control, and spend funds intended for school improvement
—Ensuring that schools can obtain high-quality instructional materials
—Maintaining a supply of high-quality sources of advice and assistance for schools
—Making sure schools have a good supply of teachers and administrators from which to choose
—Setting and putting into effect policies about teacher evaluation, promotion, and pay
—Allocating public buildings and leasing private space to ensure that every school has adequate facilities

*The immediate source of this idea is Bryk and others, *Charting Chicago School Reform: Democratic Localism as a Lever for Change* (Boulder, Colo.: Westview Press, 1997). The idea was first presented in Jane Hannaway and Lee S. Sproull, "Who's Running the Show? Coordination and Control in Educational Organizations," *Administrator's Notebook*, vol. 27, no. 9 (1978–79), pp. 1–4 .

sible for portfolio management, encouraging school development, monitoring system performance, and ensuring the quality of inputs to the school. (Minor jobs for other public and private parties such as training vendors might also be acknowledged for maintaining quality and fostering school development, but the responsibility remains with the central office).

Traditional institutional arrangements in public education maintain a hermetic seal between government-run institutions and all other organizations. Thus a city's public school system will determine what is to be taught, when, and to whom; hire all teachers and principals; buy all books and equipment; assign employees and equipment to schools; build, own, and maintain all school structures; provide in-service training to teachers; evaluate adult performance; run its own personnel system to pay, promote, and sanction staff members; assign students to schools and transport them to and from; and measure and report on its own performance. Sometimes other government agencies (public libraries and transit systems) perform important ancillary roles, and private individuals and contractors provide some professional services (legal representation, auditing, asbestos abatement, and so forth). Despite the additional services of these other agencies, the traditional public school system is a nearly pure government-operated enterprise.

The new strategies all assume that public institutions will continue to be important in education, but that some significant responsibilities will be assigned to entities outside what is now considered the public school system. Although all the strategies assume that a representative school board and related government agency will bear primary responsibility for deciding which schools will be authorized to operate with public funds, the Community Partnership option requires that these decisions be made by a broadly representative community board.

The three new strategies assume an end to the bureaucratic monopoly on workshops and courses for teacher in-service training and other forms of advice and help for school improvement. The CEO–Strong Schools strategy takes it for granted that schools will have access to any help the superintendent approves in accepting a school's annual performance and improvement plan. (In New York City District 2, Alvarado guided some schools toward assistance from the district central office, but he also helped them gain access to private assistance from as far away as Australia.) The Diverse Providers and Community Partnerships strategies are also predicated on the idea that schools will control all funds, including amounts earmarked for teacher in-service training and instructional improvement, and that they will be free to buy services from multiple sources.

All the new strategies provide that individual schools rather than the district central office will take responsibility for teacher hiring and evaluation. Even under the CEO–Strong Schools strategy, school leaders have much the same authority as the leaders of today's charter or private independent schools. School principals will work for the school and their tenure will be decided by whatever governing board the school has. Thus the central office will be unable to do what is so common in conventional public school systems—unilaterally reassign a good principal to another school or to some systemwide function. Principals thus have reason to build and stay with their schools. Based on his Chicago experience, Anthony Bryk has written, "It would be foolhardy not to structure an incentive system that encourages effective principals to make the long-term commitments necessary to transform their schools."[4]

New Roles for Nongovernmental Entities

The second and third strategies create additional roles for entities outside the government-run school system. Both assume that schools might be run by various for-profit and nonprofit entities. Under the Diverse Providers strategy, community groups, nonprofit organizations, unions, teacher cooperatives, and church-related groups would be eligible to seek licenses to run schools. The Community Partnership strategy broadens the challenge of providing services by encouraging nonschool educational and cultural organizations to supplement school offerings and requiring that city leaders attend to the out-of-school health and social service needs of low-income communities (table 5-1).

Under the CEO–Strong Schools strategy, school success and failure—and the career opportunities of teachers and principals—depend almost exclusively on judgments made by the superintendent. These judgments must be based on clear prior agreements about goals and methods, and superintendents and other public authorities must accept responsibility for allowing schools to act on these agreements. A fair criticism of many school systems' site-based management initiatives—which are intended to encourage greater school initiative without altering the basic responsibilities of the superintendent, school board, central office, and teachers' union—was that schools were forced to change their plans constantly in response to politically bargained mandates issued from above. The schools never truly had the freedom of action promised, and their performance agreements often became moot shortly after they were created.

Table 5-1. *Responsibility for Major Functions under the Current Education System and Three Alternative Institutional Arrangements*

Function	Existing system	CEO–strong schools	Diverse providers	Community partnership
Portfolio management	Superintendent, board, and bureaucracy	Superintendent	Superintendent and board	Community board
Fostering school development	Superintendent, board, and bureaucracy	Superintendent, principals, and diverse public and private assistance providers	Diverse public and private assistance providers	Private investors, churches, community groups, public and private assistance providers
Monitoring system performance	Superintendent, board, and bureaucracy	Superintendent, independent analysis agency, and inspectorate	Superintendent, board, and the choices of parents	Oversight board, choices of parents, and actions of community-based organizations
Ensuring quality inputs	Superintendent, board, and bureaucracy	Superintendent and board	Market	Market

Bryk offers a metaphor that is helpful for understanding the CEO–Strong Schools strategy. He says that it transforms a centrally operated public school system into a federation of schools.[5] In such a federation each school has a conditional warrant to receive the public's money and control the time and educational experiences of at least some of the public's children. Similarly, the central school system organization is authorized to act only to tend the portfolio of schools and protect children from failing schools.

The Diverse Providers and Community Partnership strategies create systems of accountability that include many more entities.[6] Under Diverse Providers, schools must fulfill their contracts with the school board, but they get the money they need to operate based on the number of families enrolling students. A school's contract with the school board allows it to receive public funding, but it gets money only when students enroll and bring their allocation with them. Schools use the money they receive to hire teachers, which means that they must enter a labor market in which teachers have choices and can choose to teach in schools that offer solid compensation packages, attractive work environments, and satisfying work. Thus Diverse Providers creates a true labor market for instructional and administrative staff, as does the Community Partnership strategy. Salaries would be set by the market, and schools might compete for staff by providing incentives such as a good benefits package or training programs to prospective teachers. Teachers could demand higher pay for difficult situations or heavy responsibilities, and schools could offer bonuses for strong performance.[7]

These three strategies represent three different approaches to public oversight of schools. All are intended to support and stabilize aggressive reform designs. They use different mixtures of governmental oversight, competition and entrepreneurship, family choice, and private provision of data and analysis. They can be readily arrayed on a continuum of private versus public control, but none is solely governmental or solely privatized. The CEO–Strong Schools strategy implies a government-centered plan that nevertheless leads to quasi-market competition among schools and to use of institutions independent of the school system to provide data and analysis. The Diverse Providers strategy is a classic "social market" plan in which public education is provided by diverse entities, but the basic conditions of demand and provider eligibility are set by government. The Community Partnership strategy is more a pure market system with important public oversight of the allocation of resources to schools and services.

Local circumstances and politics will inevitably affect choices among the strategies. However, mayors and others who are attracted to the CEO–Strong Schools strategy because it upsets the fewest apple carts should ask themselves whether they really mean to make the changes in locus of authority that the strategy requires. This approach eliminates school boards' ability to rule through successions of unrelated mandates. It also presumes that individuals' job rights and collective bargaining agreements will not obstruct important school improvement and redevelopment options. None of these options is consistent with the continuation of arrangements created to protect a particular bureaucracy or employee group. In all likelihood the only community that can successfully pursue the CEO–Strong Schools strategy is one that could also marshal the political initiative to choose either of the other two strategies.

The Need for New Institutions

None of the new strategies assumes that all indispensable functions can be performed by the public school system bureaucracy. First, all try to locate as much control as possible over decisions affecting instructional quality—teacher hiring and training, purchase of materials, balance between instruction and other activities, times of operation—at the school level. Second, school systems and, for that matter, individual schools have strong incentives to put all available funds into current services and therefore to neglect important investment functions—performance oversight, tracking of the supply of vital resources, creating new schools to serve neglected communities, and so forth.

In locating control over decisions at the school level, the new strategies do not assume that every school will make ideal decisions in these matters. However, schools will have strong incentives to focus time and energy on instruction, and those that fail to provide effective instruction will risk having public funds taken away and losing enrollment.[8] (The alternative, locating decisionmaking authority about spending and instruction someplace outside the school, would mean that schools would not be free to adapt to the needs of their students and could not be held fully responsible for results.) Through control of money, schools will decide what advice, services, teacher training courses, and equipment to buy. School system central offices, which under the existing system are funded via automatic set-asides over which schools have no control, would then be forced to compete for business with independent, nonprofit, university-based, and even for-profit providers.

The second reason for relying on new institutions is that school systems and individual schools regularly neglect investment functions. School boards and superintendents have strong incentives to focus on the here and now, avoid state and federal compliance actions, stay out of court, satisfy parents, and keep peace with teachers. Individual schools have strong incentives to give today's students, parents, and teachers what they need and demand. (These incentives affect private as well as public schools, as became evident in the 1970s when many Catholic schools closed because they had failed to maintain their buildings and hire new lay teachers to replace aging religious teachers.) Left to their own devices, school systems and individual schools invest too little in performance assessment and analysis of options (especially those that could prove embarrassing or create pressures to change), human resource development, innovation to adapt to changing needs, and efficient upkeep and allocation of school facilities.[9] (That is why public school systems separate capital accounts from operating funds and federal programs have provided their own set-asides for teacher training.)

The CEO–Strong Schools strategy, for example, places the responsibility for monitoring system performance in the hands of the superintendent, but it does not assume the task will be assigned to subordinate bureaucrats. The function could be, and for good reasons should be, performed by an independent analysis agency. This feature of the strategy is based on Chicago's experience in trying to build a decentralized school system. It led Bryk to make the case for quasi-public enterprises whose development would be stimulated by school board action but whose day-to-day activities would not be directly controlled by a central office.[10] Although there have been good public school system evaluation offices, in the long run no school system bureaucracy is likely to invest enough money in these functions, or to allow the most capable people to stay in research and evaluation roles when the system experiences other crises, or to publish results that will lead to criticism or demands for change.

In Chicago, whose mayor-appointed CEO exercises great power, school and system performance is assessed in numerous ways by various analysts. The most influential systemwide performance assessments are done by the Consortium on Chicago School Research, a university-based organization sponsored jointly by the city's foundations and the public school system central office. The central office provides test scores for analysis and access to schools for the consortium's surveys, but consortium leaders conduct analysis according to professional standards. Although they promise to consider school system leaders' comments about their results, consortium leaders Anthony Bryk, Penny Bender Sebring, John Q. Easton, and others ultimately decide what will be published and when. An institution similar to the Chicago Consortium could also take responsibility for analyses that traditional public school systems neglect such as tracking funds to schools to show whether schools get the amounts of real dollars they are supposed to receive for the education of particular students and analyzing the citywide distribution of teachers with outstanding qualifications.

Chicago and the Charter School Office in Massachusetts are also building independent groups of expert school visitors modeled after Her Majesty's Inspectorate of Schools in the United Kingdom. Periodic site visits are expected to stimulate school self-assessment, but the inspectors' reports can also be used in decisions about allocation of assistance resources to schools, school reconstitution, and reauthorization of charter schools.

Some observers have urged two additional forms of quasi-public enterprises. The first is a "schools' incubator" that would invest in development of new schools before they open by giving groups of school administrators and teachers a time and place to work together and receive expert help and advice long before they have to open a new school. In an incubator, groups slated to open a new school or take over an existing one can try out and choose instructional materials and approaches, plan how they will select and prepare teachers, develop materials to explain the school to parents and students, choose sources of ongoing advice and assistance, find and adapt facilities to fit the instructional program, decide how they will assess and demonstrate performance, and learn how to manage their financial and legal responsibilities.

Public school systems have seldom taken responsibility for this incubation function, and it is unlikely that they will ever do so because pressures for current services and teacher pay always outweigh the forces in favor of investment or leadership development. Existing incubators in Massachusetts and Washington State depend largely on business philanthropy but also, on occasion, charge some fees to school districts.

The second additional form of quasi-public enterprise is a public school real estate trust. Without major political or legal pressures to the contrary, regular public school systems are unlikely to make school space available to schools other than those they operate themselves. Facilities managers in some cities have told us they hoped to tear down public school structures rather than allow them to be used by competitive contract, charter, or privately run schools. If all publicly funded schools are to have the same access to publicly owned and subsidized space, someone other than the conventional district central office must control school buildings. A major foundation or business coalition could test the concept by entering an agreement with a willing medium-sized school system to form a public real estate trust. The trust would become the owner of all public school buildings and would receive all state and local funds earmarked for school construction and maintenance. The trust would maintain a stock of buildings that it would make available on a medium-term lease to all public schools, including charter and contract schools. It would sell surplus buildings and build or lease new space in areas with too many children for the space available. It would also help schools find space or help them find sublease tenants for space they no longer needed.

Distribution of Roles

One way to illustrate the core similarities among the three strategies is to review the institutional arrangements required for the CEO–Strong Schools strategy (table 5-2). The CEO–Strong Schools strategy requires important changes in the responsibilities and powers of those involved in traditional school systems. It also creates important new powers and responsibilities for principals and governing boards of individual schools,

Table 5-2. *Responsibilities of Main Entities under the CEO–Strong Schools Strategy*

Actor	Main roles
Superintendent-CEO	Advise board on all its functions; offer strategies for providing assistance to schools, ensuring that schools can choose among a supply of capable teachers and heads, using all community educational resources; manage a central services budget approved annually on a zero base
Citywide representative board	Hire and fire the CEO; authorize schools; set policies guaranteeing equitable funding for students and establishing set-asides for professional development and other extraschool functions; ratify CEO's recommendations about school closings and sanctions; enter funding and performance agreements with independent school providers
Individual school governing board or site council	Operate one school using public funds to hire administrators and teachers, and adhere to public policies on equitable access, fair treatment, and student attainment of local or state standards
Independent analysis agency	Collect management and performance data and publish annual reports on school-by-school funding, resources, strategies, and results
Independent inspectorate	Provide periodic reports on performance and needs of individual schools
Assistance providers, independent networks of allied schools	Create shared assets and improvement efforts, including professional development programs, for schools sharing instructional philosophies
Teachers' unions	Enter collective bargaining agreements with schools whose staffs choose to unionize; maintain a "hiring hall" for teachers, assist schools on teacher recruitment, provide in-service training, and mediate conflicts between schools and teachers
Teacher training institutions	Offer preservice training to enable teachers and principals to work in collaborative, coherent, and accountable schools
School incubators	Foster development of leadership teams for new and reconstituted public schools
Other educational and cultural organizations	Provide programs and services for use by all schools, public and private

and it requires creation of new institutions, some of which are partly or wholly private.

In effect, this strategy completely reshapes relationships. The superintendent, now largely subservient to boards that may be highly politicized and lack expertise, is replaced by a chief executive officer responsible for carrying out broad policy directives but reporting to multiple sources of policy guidance and possessing powerful leadership capacities to advise the board on its functions, develop and implement promising programs, and oversee school performance.

The strategy creates a citywide representative group to take on many of the policy and managerial roles of existing boards—hire the CEO, authorize schools, establish equitable funding conditions, ensure adequate funding for training and professional development, and the like. Individual school governing boards, independent analysis agencies, a new inspectorate (similar to the inspectors in England), school incubators, and teacher training institutions all contribute to the expertise available to the district and its schools.

Perhaps the most important change is contemplated for teachers' unions. Unions would be expected to enter into collective bargaining agreements not with the district but with individual schools whose teachers choose to unionize. Such a development could be contemplated only in a district in such dire straits that it had suffered the indignity of being taken over. Even in these cases, unions are normally quick to assert the sanctity of existing contracts, as they did, for example, in Washington, D.C., when Congress stepped in for a time to insist on a control board to oversee spending in city agencies generally, including the District public schools. Nevertheless, once a takeover is contemplated, various ideas for a new kind of unionism, such as hiring halls for teachers and creating new forms of professional development, become feasible.[11]

The institutional arrangements required by the CEO–Strong Schools strategy would go a long way toward supporting the other two strategies as well. However, the Diverse Providers and Community Partnership strategies require some additional arrangements, which are summarized in table 5-3.

In brief, the success of the other two strategies depends on encouraging activity by several new entities. In particular, school incubators and school real estate trusts need to be established. Meanwhile, cities would need to create mechanisms for dealing with independent and new pub-

Table 5-3. *Institutional Requirements Added by the Diverse Providers and Community Partnership Strategies*

Additional arrangements required	Principal responsibilities
School incubators	Foster development of leadership teams for new public, contract, charter, and private schools
Independent public school providers	Operate schools under agreements with school board or community board or both
Private schools	Collaborate with CEO and public schools in CEO–Strong Schools Strategy. Operate schools under agreements with school board or community board or both
Other educational, cultural, and community-based organizations	Possibly manage some schools; supplement instruction regularly; provide out-of-school supplementary experiences
Human resource agencies and community-based providers	Cooperate with community board in providing comprehensive and integrated services for children and families needing them
School real estate trust	Manage, lease, procure, and sell buildings to accommodate all schools operated with public funds

lic school providers capable of operating schools under agreement with the new communitywide education agency.

Finally, perhaps for the first time in a century, public school leaders would be forced to take into account how independent schools, other educational and cultural assets in the community, and social service providers contribute to the city's educational well-being.

New Independent Investment Needed

New institutional arrangements of the sort described in this chapter—independent analysis capability, the development of school incubators, the creation of communitywide oversight boards, and the development of networks of assistance providers—will be expensive.

Despite what many of the most critical school reform advocates aver, funds are unlikely to be discovered easily in current operations. Creating these institutional capabilities will require major new investments. Even if public funds were to become available for these purposes, they would likely be subject to ever increasing regulatory constraints or to being withdrawn suddenly in times of budget crisis or political turmoil.

Mayors and members of reform boards need to decide whether they will try to raise funds on their own or form alliances with businesses and foundations capable of supporting the new kinds of institutions that need to be built. Based on the results reported above, we are convinced that new public-private enterprises and partnerships are essential. Local philanthropies, whether controlled by businesses, individuals, or public-interest boards, must also choose between supporting day-to-day services in the schools and funding the infrastructure on which a sound community education system is based. This choice is not easy because new institutions cost money, and the case for supporting day-to-day services is often compelling. Based on back-of-the-envelope calculations, we estimate that a combination of new institutions in a community could require start-up costs as great as $5 million and ongoing annual operating costs as great as $3 million.

Chapter 6 explores these subjects. It shows that most of the needed new institutions can be created with private funds, but they will require a combination of mayoral and private initiative. It also examines regulatory and legislative changes required to make the institutions possible. The real estate investment trust will require changes in state law, as will many of the new responsibilities and missions of school boards, superintendents, and leaders of individual schools.

Chapter 6 also demonstrates that the legislative, regulatory, and financial changes are minor compared with the benefits. Private expenditures on public education of $5 million, $10 million, or even $15 million annually are small relative to the likely benefits and relative also to the amounts of money that businesses and foundations now provide for "feel good" activities that do nothing to improve system performance.

Local Politics of Reform | 6

THE DISTINCTION between strategy and implementation is central to this chapter. In the preceding chapters we discussed alternative reform strategies: coordinated actions planned with the expectation that they could make a difference in student learning. By implementation we mean what people who are supposed to put the strategy into action actually do.

Whether a strategy has the outcome intended is a result of the quality of plans made (whether they addressed real problems and took account of all the factors that determine whether a city's schools improve) and implementation (with what effort, consistency, timing, skill, and determination were plans actually put into effect?). This chapter concerns implementation. It reflects the title of the book, *It Takes a City*. Important civic leaders must become engaged in building and sustaining a reform strategy over a long time. Legitimate representatives of affected groups, especially parents and grandparents and leaders of churches and community groups in the neighborhoods most burdened by bad schools, must also be committed and influential participants.

Implementation Problems Come with the Territory

The first five chapters have detailed myriad implementation problems. Trouble putting reform in place and maintaining it is just part of the process. There is no easy way to get around these problems. An initiative that threatens no one will change little and cannot make a substantial difference in schools. A community that did not need to transform its schools would not be contemplating mayoral takeover or other major reform initiatives.

At the same time, no initiative is likely to survive if it threatens more people than it attracts, if it threatens too many people gratuitously, or if its leaders do not anticipate opposition. For a reform strategy to survive, its leaders must build as broad a coalition as is consistent with a focused initiative and either channel opposition in productive ways or meet it with countervailing ideas, organization, and political pressure.

Widespread desire for change is not enough to eliminate implementation problems. As in every other kind of enterprise, most people in a public school system hope that performance can be increased without committing to major changes in their work lives. People on school boards and in central offices, principal's offices, and classrooms know they work hard and believe that others are constantly getting in the way. It is easy for them to conclude that the key to school improvement is to change someone else's job or the way they perform it. That is why, in many poorly performing school districts, everyone wants change but every important initiative faces strong opposition.

Although opposition to reform is inevitable, it need not be intractable. Many people in the school system, including teachers and principals, sincerely believe that reform should start with someone else—fewer mandates from the school board, more funds from taxpayers, better help from the central office, and more cooperation from families and social service agencies. Heads of teachers' unions, even those that might personally think a given reform is beneficial, are still obliged to oppose initiatives that burden or upset too many of their members. However, such objections to reform are less potent when reform designs spread burdens broadly. A reform initiative backed by a powerful state takeover threat or a reconstitution mandate that would void all current contracts can also create circumstances that allow heads of teachers' unions, administrators, and school board members to cooperate.

But softening resistance is not the same thing as winning committed support. School system employees are the adults most affected by reform initiatives, and it is not realistic to expect them to change any more than the reform strategy's incentives and pressures make necessary.[1] Public school employees, including superintendents who have come up through the ranks, are accustomed to watching as new initiatives are carried out halfway and then recede. Many think a reform is implemented acceptably if a policy is announced, some money is spent, and an awards banquet is held.[2] For reform leaders, such simplistic ideas about implementation are lethal traps. Change does not become inevitable once a reform affects some "critical mass" of individuals or schools, and moral exhortation of shining examples is not enough to change entire organizations.

Thus leadership must come, strongly and for a long time, from outside the system. Superintendents are good sources of day-to-day leadership, but given their short tenures, their efforts are not enough. Leadership must come from a longer-lasting source and one that is both more deeply rooted in the community than a superintendent and less protective of the status quo than a school board or district central office.

Every community embarking on a serious reform strategy needs a long-lasting civic reform oversight group. Without such a group, whose functions and membership we discuss later, reforms are inevitably short-lived and poorly executed. Members of a civic oversight group should include the leaders of community institutions committed to the city's future, not to the interest groups that normally dominate education policy. Such a group, and the professional managers they employ, must manage the political tactics required to divert and overcome opposition and maintain community focus on a problem that many people wish would just go away.

How can such a permanent leadership group be put together? And how should it oversee the substantive and political management of implementation? Those questions are the backbone of this chapter.

Fostering Implementation

A civic reform oversight group is a community institution, not a governmental body. Formal authority to authorize and close schools, issue contracts and licenses, raise public funds, direct public spending, and set student performance must remain with elected officials and the people to whom they delegate responsibility. The civic reform oversight group ensures that these officials act openly and keeps applying pressure for rigorous implementation of the city's reform strategy.

Some might think the mayor, not some new group, is the right person to perform these functions. However, the mayor's many other responsibilities, distractions arising from other community crises, and short tenure relative to the length of time required to complete a full reform strategy imply that someone else needs to assume responsibility. The mayor's support and willingness to intervene in a crisis is essential. But the mayor cannot be expected to exercise the kind of close scrutiny or maintain the kind of firm grip on the reform's basic principles that sustaining a civic public education reform requires.

A civic reform oversight group is necessary to protect a reform design against destruction by virtually chance events—a low-turnout election that creates an antireform majority on the school board, death or retirement of a committed superintendent, or a school board's failure to make sure a new superintendent is hired with a clear mandate to continue the reform. A civic reform oversight group is an interest group, organized to protect a particular point of view, which is that a consistent reform strategy, refined in light of experience but maintained over a long time, is more likely to improve schools than a series of unrelated initiatives, each replaced before it has had time to work. The group will make sure citizens know what the reform strategy is, why it is being pursued, what it is accomplishing, and what problems must still be solved. Such a group can influence but not replace the democratic process. Though it cannot stand up against a true majority of voters in an open election fought for and against the reform, it can stabilize the reform against chance events capable of destroying its promise.

The group needs to be composed of people who are respected and influential. Potential members include former mayors and other former high officeholders (governors, congressmen, senators, judges); heads of higher education institutions, foundations, and cultural institutions (libraries, museums, performing arts centers); parents, teachers, and principals (acting on their own, not as heads of official groups); religious leaders (including heads of important African-American and other minority congregations); respected figures from the low-income and minority neighborhoods where bad schools are an urgent problem; heads of private schools; and retired CEOs. The first reform oversight group can be appointed and convened by the mayor. But the group should be self-perpetuating thereafter, and members should serve staggered terms so that it is not susceptible to abrupt changes in direction.

The group should be a quasi-public body on which members serve without pay but which has enough money to employ a small (two- or three-person) professional staff. This money should come from long-term business and foundation commitments, not from government. (Statewide reform monitoring groups in Kentucky, Washington, and Ohio have been sustained in this way. Kentucky's Pritchard Committee and its executive director Robert Sexton form one of the most potent forces in public education reform.)

The civic reform oversight group's first responsibility will be to foster development of the independent institutions discussed in previous chapters: an independent educational analysis agency, a schools inspectorate, a schools incubator, and a real estate trust to manage and lease school buildings. Few cities have such institutions, and they will require start-up capital as well as funding for their operating costs. The group should take responsibility for fund raising and for putting these new nonprofit, public-service organizations on strong legal and administrative foundations. The group can found the new institutions and provide financial help and advice with such start-up activities as preparing and filing papers to establish the organizations' legal and tax statuses, helping establish competent boards of directors, and finding qualified staff members.

The oversight group should also function as a de facto community education development foundation, raising funds from businesses, foundations, and individuals to support the new institutions over the long haul. Organizations with some such functions already exist, for example in Seattle, Portland, and Pittsburgh. They raise funds for the public school system, try to help it devise and manage major initiatives, support bond issues, and work to ensure favorable media coverage. At present these groups do not, however, provide independent oversight of reform implementation.

In any big city the private sector's most important long-term contribution to public education should be to maintain independent institutions dedicated to school quality. The necessary institutions—the civic reform oversight group, independent analysis agency, inspectorate, incubator, and real estate trust—will require substantial funding.[3] However the amounts required should not exceed the amounts that big-city businesses and philanthropies now devote to public education. In a major metropolis, including all of the nation's fifty largest cities, there are universities, business headquarters, major banks, and foundations large and small.

Although data on contributions from such sources can be difficult to find, studies completed in several localities suggest there is a great deal of money available. In Seattle, for example, businesses report donations of over $5 million a year to a school system serving barely 50,000 students. It is very unlikely that all the new institutions combined would have operating costs as high as $3 million a year, slightly more than half the $100 per student that businesses alone are now spending, often haphazardly.[4] This investment, which could have immense leverage, looks good in comparison to adding $50 per student to a public school system budget of $6,000 to $10,000 per student a year. From a business perspective, investing in the system of education in the city is a much wiser investment than tossing money at parts of the institution or even individual schools or classrooms.

Aside from founding and helping to fund new institutions, a civic reform oversight group needs to provide high-level political leadership for the city's reform strategy. Necessary functions that can be performed only by a dedicated group of senior civic leaders include

—mobilizing electoral support for the reform design;

—making sure reform strategies survive superintendent succession;

—opposing distracting proposals and pressing for termination of old arrangements;

—supporting the reform at the state capital;

—counseling school system leaders and supporting those who get into trouble for pursuing the reform;

—making sure that successes are recognized and failures lead to improvements in strategy and tactics; and

—helping build a parent constituency for reform.

Winning Elections

Community leaders must understand that school board elections are not sideshows in local politics or in carrying out a reform design. They are often the heart of local politics, and they are almost always the forums in which the entire initiative can be sustained or lost. No amount of expertise or institutional support can protect a reform initiative against a newly elected school board majority that claims a mandate to trash a strategy or fire a superintendent. School boards are not good forums for creating integrated strategy, but they are excellent platforms from which reform initiatives and their leaders can be destroyed.

Community leaders who supported Diana Lam's initiative in San Antonio or John Murphy's in Charlotte did not pay attention to the school board elections. But disaffected groups of teachers, who resented the performance pressures they had come under, did. They turned out relatively small numbers of people who controlled the elections and replaced reform supporters with opponents.

A civic reform oversight group cannot buy elections or prevent a well-mobilized majority from having its way. But it can develop an election strategy, provide public information, and manage voter turnout initiatives, all indispensable parts of reform implementation.

Surviving Succession

For a reform plan to make a significant improvement in school performance, it must persist. The typical big-city superintendent's two-and-one-half-year tenure is not long enough, nor is twice that long. Few cities can hope to keep one effective and committed superintendent for the ten or more years it may require to institutionalize the necessary changes.

The only alternative is for leaders of a civic reform oversight group to make sure successive superintendents are hired to continue and build upon, not reject and replace, the city's basic reform design. This is easier said than done. Men and women who have ascended through smaller-city superintendencies to a post in a major metropolis understand that a new superintendent has to prove himself fast by making bold and unprecedented changes. School boards typically reinforce this tendency by avoiding the hard work of hammering out agreement on priorities before advertising for a superintendent. Looking for and finding a talented individual on whom to place their hopes—preferably one who compensates for the weaknesses of predecessors—is more interesting and less upsetting than working through disagreements with fellow board members. But the consequences for continuation of a reform design can be severe.

A change in superintendents can and should be an opportunity for an honest look at what has been accomplished and open discussion of how to amend the strategy or improve its implementation. But these discussions should be overt and based on data; they must not be bypassed by a school board's decision to avoid discussion.

A civic reform oversight group needs to pay close attention to the school board's preparations to hire a new superintendent and use its moral authority and the mayor's influence to make sure that the premises on which new superintendents are hired reaffirm the city's commitment to its basic reform strategy.

Opposing Distracting Proposals and Terminating Old Arrangements

Constant, turbulent change has become the normal condition for big-city public education. Successions of boards and superintendents have left behind layers of half-implemented reforms: different categorical programs, none fully funded; different standards for teacher hiring; different and sometimes contradictory policies about the responsibilities and powers of school site councils; policies requiring alternative services for language-minority children; different polices on student discipline, truancy, and promotion; and different prescriptions about how best to group students for instruction and present new material. Each initiative lasted long enough to leave some residue of habit, policy, or staff members convinced it was the best idea that had ever come along. The premature burial of each initiative also helped convince teachers and administrators that nothing is permanent and their superiors in the administration will eternally issue new mandates but never truly make up their minds.

If a city's reform initiative is to succeed, leaders must persuade teachers and principals that it is here to stay. Rigorous plan development and a coherent approach to the city's problems will make a good start, but it will not be enough. A reform's staying power can be proved only by doing.

Reform leaders—the superintendent and school board, but especially the civic reform oversight group—can demonstrate a reform plan's staying power in two ways. First, they can resist new policies and mandates that are not demonstrably part of the reform plan; and second, they can terminate rules, administrative structures, and uses of funds that are not consistent with the reform plan. The first part of this prescription requires strong self-discipline among city leaders and the ability to be comfortable with constructive criticism. The cause of reform cannot allow them to urge every new miracle cure they hear about at national conferences or from their friends. Other city leaders must discipline their peers by demanding that new ideas be filtered back through the thinking that led to formulation of the reform plan in the first place. The standard for judgment is easy: if a new idea does not solve a problem for which city leaders were openly seeking a solution, it should not be added to the mix.

Members of school boards and civic leadership groups need to decide what the school system will no longer do, as well as what it will do in the future. All of the reform designs analyzed in the previous chapters required termination of existing central office structures, methods of allocating teachers and other resources to schools, and collective bargaining provisions that prevented schools from choosing teachers. If these underlying structures are not pulled down, no major reform plan can be built. Only a group as powerful and politically independent as the civic reform oversight group can pursue termination relentlessly enough to succeed.

Supporting Reform at the State Capital

A civic reform oversight group can help promote flexible use of funds provided by the state or passed through the state from the federal government. To promote a coherent local reform strategy, states can allow remarkably flexible use of funds from the Elementary and Secondary Education Act (ESEA), the largest federal program. Most can also help localities gain flexible interpretations of other laws and regulations, including laws normally interpreted as imposing rigid rules for education of migrant, bilingual, or disabled students.

Sometimes all that is required is that someone ask for help. Leaders of a civic reform oversight group do not have to accept the first thing they hear about what is permissible and what cannot be done. They risk less than superintendents and other school system employees when they critique the effects of rigidly enforced rules. Frequently, they also enjoy access to governors and other high state officials that superintendents and school board members do not. The civic reform oversight group should be the community's leading edge in seeking advice and cooperation from high state and federal officials, including their governor and the U.S. secretary of education.

Oversight group leaders can also help turn threats and pressures into major political resources. Threats of state takeover of a failing school system can help local interest groups and unions to put aside their differences, at least temporarily, in favor of a unified effort to retain local control. (This was evident in Cleveland, Baltimore, and Boston.) State threats to take over or close and reconstitute schools also make it possible for the local board and superintendent to take actions that would otherwise have been impossible. (This was evident in San Antonio.) Professional school system officials, accustomed to viewing state threats as pure liabilities, are less likely than senior community leaders to understand and exploit the hidden opportunities.

In the long term, however, local reform strategies will need more than waivers and accommodations from the state. They will need permanent changes in state law that allow school boards to enter performance agreements with individual schools, send all funds to schools on the basis of enrollment, and allow schools to determine their own staff structures and budgets. Collective bargaining laws must be amended to allow individual schools, not whole school systems, to employ teachers and principals, and parents must also, by law, have the right to choose any publicly funded school for their child.

Initiative for such laws might come from the governor or state legislative leaders, but it might not. State education policymaking is often heavily influenced by the needs of suburbs and rural areas, where school performance is less likely to fall to low enough levels to motivate fundamental change. A civic reform oversight group speaking for a major city should have little difficulty successfully advocating needed changes in state law.[5]

Counseling Reform Superintendents and Union Leaders

In addition to providing electoral support, a civic reform oversight group must help the superintendent or other chief executive officer charged with day-to-day management of reform survive the inevitable tensions with groups defending the status quo. In the course of carrying out a reform, superintendents must sometimes decide to reassign poorly performing or intransigent staff, eliminate programs that some community members like, reallocate dollars, and revise use of facilities. This can lead to an accumulation of political burdens and has on more than one occasion led opponents to support antisuperintendent factions in school board campaigns.

There are two ways senior community leaders can help a pro-reform superintendent avoid becoming the issue in a school board campaign. First, they can present controversial actions in context, showing the public why these actions must be taken and how they will advance the reform plan. Second, they can counsel superintendents to avoid needless dramatization and personalization of issues. With this kind of advice, some competent superintendents who were committed to plausible reform strategies might have maintained their positions instead of losing them.

Following are examples of ways civic reform oversight groups can counsel superintendents.

—Superintendents can avoid confrontation with teachers' unions by taking advantage of the retirement of nearly half the public school teaching force in the next five years. This makes it unnecessary for anyone to lose his or her job because of a reform program. Superintendents can say that people who cannot measure up to the challenges of a reform design may have to be reassigned to less responsible jobs, and some might become disenchanted and seek other employment. But no one needs to be fired.

—School closing, which has become an issue that few superintendents or school boards can handle, might be unnecessary. This does not mean, however, that local reform strategies should not set out to transform the local supply of public schools. Leaders of a civic reform oversight group can counsel the superintendent to charter one or more small competing schools in neighborhoods now served by failing schools and make it clear that parents can decide where to enroll their children. Competition and continued assistance can often turn a troubled school around. Failing that, the slow departure of families can encourage staff members to leave a failing school and reduce the strength of opposition if it ultimately closes.

A civic reform oversight group can also provide cover for reformist union leaders. Some of the most potent opposition to reform can come from teacher groups, but so can some of the most important leadership. Union leaders Tom Mooney (Cincinnati), Roger Erskine (Seattle), Adam Urbanski (Rochester), Pat Tornillo (Miami), and the late Helen Bernstein (Los Angeles) have been among the most imaginative and courageous architects for their districts' reforms. These and other leaders have supported reform at some risk to their own positions, especially from leaders of teacher factions which, preferring the traditional division between labor and management, resist movement toward a more competitive, performance-based system.

Union heads who favor reform usually try to lead members by arguing that change is inevitable and it is better for the union to get ahead of it than be dragged along. They have natural allies among teachers and among those who think the current rule-bound public education system is not good for teachers or students. But reformist leaders and their within-union allies can be seriously undermined not only by recalcitrant members but also by shifting school board policies and inconsistent actions by superintendents. When the school board vacillates or strong superintendents are replaced by more timid ones, union leaders can be isolated and at risk for their jobs.

Leaders of a civic reform oversight group should foster a consistent policy climate and make sure that union leaders can rely on promises made. No one should be lulled into thinking union leaders are irrevocably committed to reform. They work for organizations dedicated to maximizing teacher pay, making working conditions as pleasant as possible, and controlling entry to the teaching profession to limit competition. But there are important areas of shared interest, and city leaders should cooperate fully with union leaders who are willing to acknowledge and act on these.

Making Sure Successes Are Acknowledged and Failures Lead to Action

Bold reform strategies polarize opinion between those who think any change is desirable and those who resist and fear the motives behind any outside pressure on the public education establishment. To be fully implemented, a reform strategy needs to be tended by somebody in the middle who will both insist on the necessity of reform and press to acknowledge and learn from failures.

Superintendents and politicians favoring reform have difficulty acknowledging failures, and they often resist exposing reform implementation to close scrutiny. Opponents of reform often take advantage of the resulting information gap to publish biased accounts of what is happening and who is being hurt. A civic reform oversight group can make sure that information serves the cause of reform and evidence of problems leads to corrective action.

We have already cited the example of the Consortium for Chicago School Research, which has conducted hard-nosed assessments of whether reform initiatives are having their intended effects on schools. A mixture of good and bad news has forced city leaders and educators to continually strengthen the city's reform strategy. As a result, Chicago leaders have not enjoyed many periods of blissful confidence that their initiatives will magically transform the schools. But they do have a living, improving reform strategy.

The information for such continual reassessment of reform progress can come from the independent reform monitoring institutions discussed earlier in this chapter. The mature consideration of how to interpret and act on that information should come from the civic reform oversight group.

Building a Parent Constituency

Finally, but not least important, a civic reform oversight group needs to build a broad constituency for the reform plan, especially among parents. Groups that oppose the plan, especially dissident teachers, can tell stories about its consequences (for beloved teachers, for whether students will be cast out of their neighborhood schools, for whether some other ethnic group is about to seize control of the most important neighborhood institution) that can turn parents against it.[6] Such lurid tales are hard to eradicate once they are spread and believed. City leaders have to seek a grassroots constituency from the beginning and be prepared to quell false rumors as soon as they arise.

A continuing function of a civic reform oversight group must be to provide parent-friendly explanations of the reform, and make sure parents are never surprised about what is coming and how their own children's schools will be affected. In every case, the group's goal should be to avoid having to mount defensive campaigns against rumors by telling the story first and providing the framework in which parents give and receive information.

Moving from Square One

These political prescriptions can be daunting. They definitely involve senior civic leaders in a long-term campaign of educational, financial, administrative, and political change. The implicit message is clear: reform of failed big-city education systems is for the desperate and the determined, not the faint of heart. Once city leaders take responsibility, they must be prepared to keep it for a long time.

A civic reform oversight group acting on these prescriptions can do a great deal to ensure that a reform design works as intended. Effective, lasting reform will require constant tending. But the alternative is to go back every few years and start over to do it again. In the future, Brookings will report in greater detail about how these oversight groups can operate and how the four new institutions we recommend they sponsor should be set up and operated.

The final chapter returns to square one. When a mayor or group of city leaders find themselves in charge of a failed school system, how do they get started? How do they move from square one to the enviable but challenging position assumed by this chapter of a civic reform oversight group that has a coherent reform plan and needs only to ensure that it is rigorously implemented?

Getting Started 7

CHAPTERS 4, 5, AND 6 provide ideas about how community leaders can create and sustain a long-term strategy to improve public education in a big city. This concluding chapter returns to the beginning, to the questions that mayors and other city leaders will inevitably ask when they realize that their public school system is not going to improve enough on its own and that intervention is necessary.

Ideally, this realization should come before a crisis forces an immediate takeover. Unfortunately, some takeovers (in Baltimore and Washington, D.C.) have come suddenly as entities outside the community (the Maryland state legislature in the case of Baltimore and Congress in the case of the District of Columbia) suddenly reached a consensus. Civic and business leaders in virtually all major cities, including those analyzed in earlier parts of this book, need to be alert to the possibility that the reform initiatives tried so far will collapse and new, bolder strategies will be necessary.

How do city leaders recognize the possibility of takeover, and once takeover is imminent what steps can they take? Some basic prescriptions are clear. Mayors and city leaders should at least track the performance of the public school system. Does the real dropout rate for minority students (the proportion of students who enter seventh grade but do not graduate from high school six or even eight years later) hover near 50 percent? Does the system include a high proportion (15 percent or more) of schools in which, for five years or longer, less than one-third of the students are performing at grade level? Are there more than one or two elementary schools in which the majority of African-American or Hispanic students routinely fall behind in reading by the fourth grade? Simple questions like these will identify a school system that can easily be tagged for takeover by a legislature, court, or mayor concerned about the consequences of a weak human resources base for the city's future.

In monitoring school system performance, city leaders should watch what actually happens in the schools, not what central office leaders say should be happening. Leaders of the city's public school system might not be entirely candid about the schools' performance, not because they are dishonest but because they have convinced themselves that the latest action will solve the problem. So we find school leaders actively involved in trying to make things better by announcing new initiatives, raising standards, creating new academic programs, launching programs to make teachers smarter and happier, and investigating many other possibilities. But school systems continually churn through these new initiatives without noticeable effect. Conscientious city leaders will support, not attack, such efforts, but they should not be lulled into complacency that "this one will surely work."[1] City leaders should watch performance, not policy churn.[2] They should also spend—probably through a local development-oriented business committee—the few thousand dollars necessary for an independent consultant to analyze school system and state data on citywide dropout rates and the performance of individual schools.

Once a takeover becomes imminent (it may be suggested as a remedy in a civil suit about school performance or as a legislative proposal under consideration by the governor or state legislature), local leaders should prepare themselves for the eventuality. Leaders who wait until a takeover is upon them to define the problem and consider first steps are unlikely to create a workable reform strategy.

The remainder of this chapter makes simple suggestions about how community leaders, either anticipating or facing a takeover, can get started, and how they can get help.

How to Get Started

Any preparation for a takeover, however remote the possibility, should start with answers to three questions. In what ways is public school performance now a problem for the city? Why haven't past reform efforts succeeded? What relevant local assets are not now engaged in the effort to improve schools?

The first question is important because it sets the scope of the problem: Is it localized in a few neighborhoods or is it systemwide? The second question helps identify the barriers—lack of technical or administrative capacity or some stakeholders' dogged resistance to change—that future reform strategies must overcome. The third question is important because it helps identify sources of expertise, instructional ideas, and assistance to schools that might exist in colleges, universities, private school systems, software companies, research centers, foundations, business training organizations, and other local institutions, public and private. City leaders should seek their own answers to these questions by using special task forces (for example, of the local civic committee or business roundtable) or hiring an independent consultant.

In seeking an answer to the first question, fundamental data on basic school performance are essential. Which groups of students are not being well prepared? What proportion of the city's future labor force is unlikely to be able to read, perform simple mathematics computation, or manage their own futures as earners? What are the likely social and economic effects of continuing the school system's current level of performance?

In seeking answers to the question about the fates of past reform initiatives, brief histories of recent attempts are indispensable. City leaders will be surprised to see how many new education reforms have been announced in the past five or ten years and how each was ultimately abandoned before it had a significant effect at the school level. In as small and placid a city as Seattle there were three major reform initiatives (a citywide strategic plan for improvement, a "vanguard schools" experiment with lump-sum school-based budgeting, and local parent-teacher site councils to create school-specific improvement plans) in the five years preceding the plan summarized in chapter 2. After these plans were proudly announced and brochures were printed, each was quietly abandoned and given a decent burial. The reasons were manifold: difficulties in gaining union or central office cooperation, confusion about whether state or federal funds could be used as the new initiative implied, disagreement on the school board about the range of decisionmaking permissible at the school level, or the superintendent's inability to schedule promised school visits and meetings.

Knowing in advance what has killed past programs will help city leaders anticipate sources of resistance to future ones. They will also gain a much deeper understanding of which stakeholders have a habit of endorsing plans enthusiastically in public while effectively hamstringing implementation behind closed doors.

Local leaders also need to assess the quality of information available about basic school system management processes. Most will find that school systems lack information that is routinely available to businesses. Except in Tennessee, no urban district is able to link annual changes in students' academic growth to placements in a particular school or classroom. Few school systems know how many teachers they will have to recruit in the next five years or where their new teachers will come from or from which colleges and universities their best and worst teachers normally come. Few systems can answer similar questions about recruitment, training, and performance of school principals. Nor do many urban districts have well-defined recruitment strategies for newly trained teachers, mid-career people who would like to try teaching, or teachers who quit to raise children but are ready to return to the classroom.

The list of data deficiencies is nearly endless. Few urban school systems can say exactly how much money is spent on individual schools, how much variation in spending per pupil is created by allowing senior teachers to cluster in schools in the wealthier neighborhoods, or how much money is available for teacher training scattered in many small accounts throughout the budget. Some, but not many, districts have tracked the effects of individual principals on parent satisfaction and student performance. Local leaders should make sure such information is available, either by helping school district employees assemble data and prepare analyses routinely or by contracting with data management firms.

Aside from these analyses of the scope of the problem, local leaders need to begin to discuss the premises on which any future reform strategy should be based. Some elements of that discussion will be pleasant and interesting. Local leaders should ask local and national educational leaders (including heads of colleges and universities, museums and libraries, and respected private schools) to meet with them and discuss significant questions.

—If you could set aside all constraints, what kinds of schools would you want?

—What kind of teaching and learning do you expect?

—Whom does the district need to serve? (And whom does it serve least well?)

—Where is the district doing a good job with children who are normally at risk?

—How might this success be reproduced elsewhere?

Once a takeover is imminent, the mayor or other local leaders who will assume responsibility for the school system need to initiate much more specific and urgent deliberations. The executive charged with responsibility for the school system should assemble an independent takeover team staffed by university and business consultants as well as one or two senior staff members from the school system. This team must provide the mayor or other local executive with two kinds of analysis: a basic administrative and data reconnaissance and a political map.

The administrative and data reconnaissance should answer questions like the following.

—From what sources does the school district derive income (local, state, federal, philanthropic), and what constraints do different funding sources impose?

—How much money is spent at the school system central office (whether or not funds are spent for services done on behalf of schools)?

—What proportion of all the district's staff works in the central office or is not directly under the supervision of school principals? What is the real dollar annual cost of the district's extraschool structure?

—How much does real-dollar funding per pupil vary from school to school, and what causes the variation?

—What rules prevent allocation of funds to schools on a real-dollar per pupil basis?

—Where have past school funding increases been spent? What caused them to be spent in those ways?

—How much money is spent for student transportation, and how much of that total is spent transporting children from the neighborhoods of poorly performing schools to better-performing schools?

—What state laws and regulations apply to the size or composition of the central office and the use of funds for specific functions such as transportation?

—What rules determine where students attend school, and what rules prevent parents in low-income and minority neighborhoods from sending their children to schools in other neighborhoods?

—What central office programs, offices, and funds are now devoted to creating schooling options for low-income and minority children?

—How are decisions about adoption of textbooks, instructional materials, and teacher training made? To what extent do these decisions reflect school initiative rather than that of the central office?

—What does the current teachers' union contract provide about teacher recruitment and assignment? How does the contract constrain the allocation of funds to schools?

—Who controls school buildings and what rules constrain the assignment of underused school space?

—What funds for school construction and renovation are available, and how closely aligned are facilities plans with the districts' initiatives for instructional improvement?

—How is the student population changing? Is there a mismatch between location of facilities and population?

—In what neighborhoods have parents given up on the public schools?

This political map should identify stakeholders and their agendas. These should include the school board, teachers' and administrators' unions, permanent officials in the central office, parent groups, and habitual donors of funds and equipment. What do these people favor? What have they opposed or sabotaged in the past? What options would they demand be taken off the table from the start? By what tactics might the mayor or other leaders keep those options on the table at least until it is clear what reforms should be considered? (In most cities the most important issues to be kept on the table concern teacher hiring and assignment. Unless these can become variables in a reform strategy, changes in instruction and school performance are unlikely.)

Aside from these basic reconnaissance activities, leaders responsible for takeovers should also start by announcing a number of principles for further action. Based on past corporate and public sector transformations, we recommend that these principles be established from the beginning.

First, the reform strategy will not organize anyone out of a job. People's job assignments might change, jobs in direct contact with students will be emphasized, and everyone will be required to perform. But the reform strategy will not be based on a job purge. (Such a pledge will reduce resistance based on fear. In an environment where school systems are unable to fill principal and teacher vacancies, it is not an expensive promise to make.)

Second, the reform strategy will include fair trials of multiple ideas. Rather than defining reform as an effort to create a single districtwide initiative from the beginning, local leaders should make it clear that reform will explore multiple ideas and give each of them a fair shot at success. So the reform might consider chartering schools in some neighborhoods, using the New American Schools design in others, and reconstitution in yet different communities. This approach should blunt the winner-take-all character of traditional school system politics and send the message that no group can block a trial just because they would not like to see the idea used throughout the district.

Third, responsibility for day-to-day operations will be split off from planning and carrying out the reform strategy. To prevent the mayor and other city leaders from being drowned in immediate crises (and from making short-term decisions that foreclose potentially desirable options), day-to-day operational duties should be assigned to a conservator. Planning the reform strategy, including designing neighborhood-based trials, should proceed for a year before the takeover team assumes daily responsibility for school operations.

How to Get Help

Every locality will have to create its own strategy. Local politics, history, and institutional capacities must be considered, and there is no substitute for committed local leadership. However, no reform leader needs to be entirely a captive of local people and organizations. All should seek help from national organizations, which can apply lessons from other localities and also suggest lines of action that might not be identified through local deliberative processes.

Mayors and others responsible for takeovers or other major interventions in a city school system should use one or more of the available national resources. These include:

—the Education Commission of the States' (ECS) National Commission on Governing America's Schools, which offers assistance to states and localities contemplating takeovers and other major reform initiatives.[3]

—the Consortium for Policy Research in Education (CPRE), based at the University of Pennsylvania and Harvard University, which studies urban reform strategies and is engaged in an experimental takeover in San Diego.[4]

—the Urban School Reform program at Brookings, which has produced this book and will soon publish a separate review of school system databases and what must be done to create community-based analytic capacities to support fundamental reform initiatives.[5] The Brookings program also collaborates with ECS on advising mayors and other city leaders charged to take over failing urban school systems.

Conclusion

This book has provided examples of reform initiatives in cities trying to reverse decades of poor performance, particularly among schools serving low-income and minority youth. It has also suggested bolder strategies than any yet tried and has outlined political and administrative tactics for making sure reform strategies once designed will actually be put into practice. It does not paint a pretty picture, either of the condition of city school systems or what must be done.

It has taken the better part of the twentieth century to create city public systems that are as inflexible and careless about quality as the ones we have. As the preceding chapters demonstrate, city leaders have something to build on, but not a lot. In most cities the problem is a fundamental one of supply. We have too few good schools, and many of the others must be replaced with new organizations built to be effective. We have too few good teachers and administrators, and the others must be replaced by people trained (or retrained) to work in and support high-performance, accountable schools.

The problems of big-city school systems need solutions that improve human resources, strengthen and sometimes recreate institutions, and channel political energies away from adult financial interests and toward student learning. The strategies we have outlined have all these elements. But they are complex, and putting them into practice will be difficult.

Sensible men and women, mayors, business leaders, foundation heads, and educators will ask whether they have to expose themselves to all the pain and turbulence that effective strategies for the reform of city schools will impose. If they look closely at city schools, these same people will conclude that they must either endure the stresses now or face even more dire problems in the future.

Appendix:
Case Studies
of Six Cities

IN 1998 the Center on Reinventing Public Education at the University of Washington conducted six case studies on urban school districts that were carrying out school reforms. The cities were chosen based on their national reputations as places trying out bold and promising new ideas for citywide education reform.

The cities selected were Boston, Memphis, New York City's District 2, San Antonio, San Francisco, and Seattle. Each city was visited twice over the course of six months by teams of researchers based at the University of Washington. Thorough reviews of written research, media sources, and district documents were conducted before the visits. Researchers visited each city for three to ten days and interviewed up to twenty-seven people involved in the reforms in each. (The exception to these methods was District 2, which was the subject of many concurrent studies. The researcher conducted a meta-analysis of others' work and visited the city once to keep from burdening administrators and teachers.) Table A-1 provides further detail on each city.

Researchers did not use a formal research instrument but followed fairly clear guidelines to explore the nature of the reform, its theories of action and what it set out to do, and its strengths and weaknesses. The

Table A-1. *Basic Details on Six Cities and School District Case Study Methodology*

City	Site visit	Number of interviews	District size	Superintendent
Boston	February 1998 August 1998	18	63,000 students, 128 schools	Thomas Payzant
Memphis	April 1998 November 1998	27	112,000 students, 162 schools	Gerry House
New York City District 2	March 1998 August 1998	Many interviews and data from published sources	22,000 students, 48 schools (no high schools)	Anthony Alvarado[a]
San Antonio	May 1998 October 1998	22	60,700 students, 95 schools[b]	Diana Lam[a]
San Francisco	February 1998 November 1998	12	61,000 students, 116 schools	Waldemar Rojas[a]
Seattle	February 1998 August 1998	19	47,500 students, 97 schools	John Stanford[a]

a. No longer leading this district.
b. 1996–97 school year.

interviews were meant to get a sense from the superintendent about the reform and to corroborate that understanding with others inside and outside the district.

Far from setting out to criticize, we set out to document the reform efforts under way because they appeared to be among the most ambitious and promising in place. What quickly became apparent, however, was that reforms that appeared to be robust and flourishing from afar turned out up close to be struggling and were frequently a bone of serious political contention locally.

BOSTON PUBLIC SCHOOLS

In 1995 the conditions for systemic reform in Boston were excellent. The new superintendent, Thomas Payzant, described as the "dean of superintendents—one of the brightest lights among the nation's educators" arrived in October.[1] The financial resources were in place; the state and municipal economies were strong. The political will was there: Mayor Thomas M. Menino had taken the rare stance of resting his political legacy on the success of the city's schools. The school board, which became an appointed rather than elected body under Menino's administration, was making decisions unmarred by internal strife. The relationship between the Boston Teachers Union and management was better than it had been in decades. In sum, the stars were aligned. If there was ever a time for major educational reform in Boston, 1995 was it.

But three years into Payzant's tenure the pressure was mounting to see results. Mayor Menino announced in his reelection address on January 6, 1998, "This is no time for business as usual. . . . To the schools I say: Your actions had better be ambitious."

Case Study

This case study describes the Boston strategy, its history, and its main features. It then summarizes the key elements of the reform strategy in terms of significant assets on which the Boston reform can draw and the unresolved issues standing between Payzant and the reforms he and his team have put in place.

The case study was developed through a two-part process:

—interviews conducted by a Boston-based education researcher in February and August 1998 with the superintendent, administrators, union leaders, principals, teachers, parents, students, and community and business leaders; and

—a review of public documents describing Boston's reform plans and a variety of news reports about the progress of those plans.

The Payzant Administration

Thomas Payzant was received in Boston with high expectations. He was a native of Massachusetts and an experienced educator with a national reputation. At the time of his appointment he was the U.S. Department of Education's assistant secretary for elementary and secondary education, and he had been the superintendent of schools in Eugene, Oregon (1973–78), Oklahoma City, Oklahoma (1979–82), and San Diego, California (1982–93).[2]

Payzant's senior management team has grown and changed. In 1995 Janice Jackson, who had served with him in the Department of Education, was his sole deputy. After three years, Jackson left Boston Public Schools and Payzant increased his senior management team from two to five. In an interview the superintendent said of Jackson,

> She and I worked as a team. We didn't have anybody in between us and the principals in terms of supervision and evaluation. What we found was that we were getting bogged down in a lot of the day-to-day work . . . which took away from the time we wanted to spend on teaching and learning issues. . . . [Ultimately, we decided] we really couldn't provide the effective support and evaluation these 128 principals needed.

In Jackson's place, Payzant created four new positions. Michael Contompasis, headmaster of the Boston Latin School for the previous nineteen years, became chief operating officer, overseeing human resources, budget, and operations. Timothy Knowles, formerly team leader for teaching and learning, began as deputy superintendent for teaching and learning, overseeing the standards and assessment systems as well as managing student and parent support services. Bak Fun Wong, a former principal of the Josiah Quincy Upper School and leader of one of the school system's clusters of schools , took over as deputy superintendent for clusters and school leaders; Amalia Cudeiro-Nelson became his assistant deputy. Together they support and evaluate the system's principals.

Demographics

Boston, the nation's oldest school district, looks like a typical mid-sized urban district. It has 63,000 students and 128 schools (17 are high schools).[3] Bilingual students make up 17 percent of the population and one in five students is labeled Special Needs. African Americans make up 49 percent of the school population, followed by Latinos (26 percent), Caucasians (16 percent), and Asians (9 percent).[4]

Standardized test scores have been mixed. In 1995 Metropolitan Achievement Test scores showed that students were, on average, performing around the 50th percentile nationally (slightly higher in the elementary grades and slightly lower in high school). After 1995 the Boston public schools switched to the Stanford 9 Achievement Test on the premise that it was a more rigorous assessment.[5] The 1997 test scores on the Stanford 9 in reading and mathematics revealed that although, on average, students in third grade were performing at or above the national median, students in all other grades tested (fifth, sixth, seventh, ninth, and eleventh) performed below the national median. High school students performed the worst, with only 6 percent of the students at a proficient level in math.

In addition, there are substantial gaps in performance when scores are disaggregated by race.[6] From 1985 to 1995 seventh grade black students' scores went from 22 percentage points behind seventh grade white students to 33 points behind. There are similar gaps at other grade levels.

Despite generally low numbers, however, the trend from 1996 to 1999 has been positive. Test scores in the elementary grades have risen incrementally.

The Strategy

Payzant described Boston's reform strategy as an "intersection of internal and external forces." It is a standards-based reform effort merged with a Whole School Change model. To understand this strategy, it is important to understand its evolution. The development of Boston's strategy can be captured in three stages: state reform efforts, Payzant's vision, and the Annenberg influence.

State Reform Efforts

Before Superintendent Payzant's arrival in 1995, the state established some important preconditions. The Education Reform Act of 1993 mandated the creation of the state's first academic standards and high-stakes assessments. It also required that school-site councils be established in every school and that lifetime teacher certification be eliminated. Thus a framework for standards-based reform, school-level control, and teacher accountability was in place.

Payzant's Vision: Focus on Children

Superintendent Payzant's vision involves a trade-off of greater autonomy at the school level in exchange for increased centralized accountability. Before accepting the superintendent position in Boston, he wrote,

> Challenging expectations for all students and employees should be established and results monitored centrally, but individual schools should be given flexibility through shared decision-making to determine how best to use their resources to meet district standards. The quid pro quo for school autonomy is accountability for results. Such an organization will require a streamlined central office.[7]

Payzant's reorganization plan reflected this vision. The traditional organizational pyramid was inverted: school-site councils were on top and the district central administration was at the bottom. The district shifted its focus from "compliance and control to support and service." To increase communication between the schools and the central office, Payzant removed a layer of central office administrators and divided the system's 127 schools into 10 clusters. A principal in each was appointed to be a cluster leader and charged with serving as a liaison between the schools and the district. These cluster leaders serve on his leadership team and meet with him regularly.

Payzant's five-year reform plan, Focus on Children, is based on high standards for all students. The goal is, he said, to create a "good *system* of schools that is focused on teaching and learning." The public schools made a commitment to investing in targeted professional development because "people are our most valuable resource." In addition, Boston created its own Citywide Learning Standards, switched to a more rigorous standardized test, and phased in performance-based assessment requirements at all grades in all subject areas.

Annenberg Challenge and Whole School Change

In 1996 the Annenberg Foundation awarded the Boston Public Schools a challenge grant: it challenged the city's private and public sectors to raise $20 million for school reform. If they did, the foundation would match their donations with $10 million. Six months later the city's corporations and foundations had exceeded their $10 million goal, and the city committed an additional $10 million in new public funds over four years.[8]

That same year the public school system worked with the Boston Plan for Excellence, a local education foundation, to create what is referred to as Whole School Change (WSC), in which a school chooses an instructional focus and works with a coach to use student performance data to drive decisions regarding resource allocation (human, time, and financial) in the hope of maximizing teaching and learning.[9] More specifically, WSC is meant to have the following components:

—Identify and use schoolwide instructional focus to meet students' needs;

—Look at student work and data in relation to the Citywide Learning Standards to identify students' needs, to improve assignments and instruction, to assess student progress, and to inform professional development;

—Create a targeted professional development plan that gives teachers and principals what they need to improve instruction in core subjects;

—Learn and use best teaching practices;

—Look at human, time, and monetary resources and align them with the instructional focus;

— Involve parents and the community in the citywide learning standards and assessments and introduce ways parents and the community can support students.[10]

The Boston Plan for Excellence launched the first cohort of twenty-seven schools, called 21st Century Schools, in 1996, and since then Annenberg and the school system have begun working with the remaining three cohorts.[11]

In sum, Boston's strategy has evolved. Although it is still essentially a standards-based reform effort, it is now driven at the local level by "instructional leadership teams" made up of small groups of teachers and their WSC coaches. (School-site councils still exist, but appear to be less important in the Whole School Change strategy.) These teams assess the test data provided by the central office and use the information to make decisions about how to allocate their school's fiscal and human resources. Clusters contain schools at various stages of reform and thus serve as vehicles for communication among schools and between the schools and the district. The district office's responsibility is to support the schools via professional development and to hold them accountable for results.

Key Assets for Reform

There appear to be three primary assets working in favor of this reform: the direction of a nationally recognized leader, broad community support, and a clear focus on achievement.

A Nationally Recognized Leader

Payzant is an educator and a superintendent admired for his vision and patience. The citizens, educators, and leaders of Boston were thrilled that he wanted to come to the city and put his careful and experienced effort into local public school reform. His national reputation may help the reform maintain its momentum. Even his detractors respect him, and the media have continued to back his steady approach even when test scores did not improve immediately. Payzant's national status may give Boston's reform effort the time and space it needs to flourish.

Broad Community Support

Boston has always been a strong supporter of public education. In fact, Neil Sullivan, executive director of the Boston Private Industry Council, said that the business, labor, and political communities were working for over a decade in preparation for "a Payzant to come along." When the superintendent arrived, a progressive labor contract was in place, and the business and foundation worlds were ready to invest.

Focus

Payzant has brought to his reforms an insistence on the need to focus on teaching and learning. He wants the message to be clear and consistent. He began his meeting with principals in the fall of 1997 by holding a copy of the Citywide Learning Standards over his head and saying, "same standards, same strategy, year two."

This focus on teaching and learning serves as an overarching strategy under which the district and schools can align their resources. At the district level, Payzant spoke to Boston's foundations and requested that any of their contributions be made in alignment with the district's strategy. In addition, the district sponsored an analysis of their school-level spending patterns to increase the efficiency of resource allocations at the local level. Ultimately, the district hopes to develop a resource guide to help principals maximize their federal and state funding. Mary Russo, a principal in Boston and the director of the Annenberg Challenge, said Whole School Change is inspiring principals to make budgetary decisions on what will improve student learning rather than on favoritism or what she calls "projectitis."

> It's a value shift. It's about looking at needs in terms of instruction rather than 'I have to take care of this and that person because she's loyal to me.' It's also about moving away from 'projectitis.' In the past, you were a good administrator if you could pull in as many grants as possible [but] the problem was that you'd end up with a grab bag full of projects and you'd use the money for whatever you needed and there was no focus, so we didn't see any improvements.

Having a clear mission has enabled the district to broaden the scope of its reform efforts while maintaining its cohesiveness. For example, the Boston Public Schools (BPS) have launched a range of new initiatives— a campaign for increased attendance, tougher promotion standards, and an effort to reduce the performance gap among blacks, Latinos, and whites—but because these are all consistent with the idea of improving teaching and learning, they appear to be deepening rather than watering down the reform's impact.

Even critics of this administration's efforts have acknowledged that they have been focused. Hubie Jones, of the Critical Friends Group, asserted that the superintendent has "done a good job at keeping the noise at bay."

Challenges to the Reform

The success of the reforms also lie in the ability to create alignment, capacity, and accountability in a relatively short time. The synergy of this mix of assets and challenges appears to be important in the long-term success of this reform effort.

Alignment

Although reform efforts appear to be focused in Boston, they are not always well aligned. There is little alignment between the district's Citywide Learning Standards and the off-the-shelf Stanford 9 assessments. Similarly, there is a lack of alignment among district and state standards and assessments. Tim Knowles, now deputy superintendent for teaching and learning, pointed out that the state was pushing the district's reforms.

> We are trying to keep the message simple: high standards for all kids, but we have to move at a particular pace to prep for [the state test]. We're incrementally focusing on one subject at a time but have to move fast to prepare for the state test. The state is driving the agenda to an extent, the schools are overwhelmed, but we need to keep moving forward. It's frustrating because we are bound by this test and it may or may not be any good.

Another issue of alignment deals with how decisions are made at the school level. An important part of the Boston strategy is that schools will use the test data they get from the central office to make funding and curricular decisions. However, who should be making those decisions is not always clear. Currently, a school could have a site council, an Annenberg instructional leadership team, and a Fleet Bank leadership team in their building.[12] How well these decisionmaking bodies work in concert will likely have a bearing on how effectively student performance data are used by the schools.

There also appears to be a lack of alignment in the central office with the district's espoused vision. The BPS reorganization plan called for a cultural shift "away from control and compliance and toward service and support." Yet aside from upper management, the compliance structure of the central office appears to have remained largely unchanged. Further, how the expertise across functional groups can be used most efficiently is still being worked out. For example, Payzant acknowledged, "there are certain cross-cutting functions, like professional development, which could certainly benefit from the expertise of our teaching and learning team, but we haven't figured out how organizationally we can best use all of our [internal resources] to support the schools."

Capacity

Shifting more power from the central office to schools required that principals take on more responsibility than they may have been ready for. "Many principals were never expected to be instructional leaders in a direct sense," Payzant said in an interview. "Rather, they were expected to be managers and problem solvers in logistical and operational matters. It is a major shift, and why everything we are doing in terms of leadership development is based around instructional leadership."

For some principals this transformation has been overwhelming. One suggested that she did not know what to do with all this new information, and that even if she did know how to analyze it, she did not feel she could make the personnel changes she wanted. Payzant countered by saying, "Principals have more authority to make changes than they sometimes believe they do. Largely they don't do it because it's very difficult when 90 percent of your budget is in people, and in order to make changes, you've got to change people. . . . It's often hard to have the conversation."

A more general capacity issue is finding and training qualified teachers. Fifty percent of the BPS teaching force will be eligible for retirement in the next decade. Payzant has hired a chief operating officer to create a comprehensive human resource system and described it this way:

> One of the major things we need to do is develop a thoughtful human resources strategy for the whole system that will prepare us to take the organization of 8,000 employees and 64,000 kids into the next century. I am talking about the *whole* system—hiring, evaluating, training, all the way through to termination—whether it's the result of thirty-five years of wonderful service or termination because the person is not meeting standards and should be dismissed.

Accountability

Although BPS has developed standards and measurement tools, it is just beginning to implement the consequences associated with failure to meet those standards. For example, teacher evaluations were first established in the 1983 Boston Teachers Union contract, and in the past two school years, 97 percent of the 3,419 teachers who were evaluated either exceeded or met expectations. During this time no permanent teachers were dismissed, and only 17 provisional teachers were let go because of performance.[13] Payzant asserts further that rather than retraining or dismissing bad teachers, principals often pass them on to someone else in the system, what he referred to as "the dance of the lemons." He is aware of this problem and has assigned a task force to address teacher evaluation and support. This low turnover and slow response are occurring in a system in which more than one out of every four ninth graders do not make it to graduation.[14]

At the level of principal, Payzant suggests there has been a lot more "movement." He estimates that in the past three years approximately 25 percent to 30 percent of the principals have left their positions through a combination of nonrenewal of contracts, retirements, promotions, and resignations. However, he points out that training the people he has is much more efficient than moving them out.

The 1998–99 academic year was the first year the system's comprehensive accountability policy was in place. Maryellen Donahue, director of the Office of Research, Assessment, and Evaluation, asserted that accountability at all levels will be "data driven." Data will not only be defined by test scores but by various student and school performance measures. Specifically, BPS will begin site visits of schools similar to those carried out by the British inspectorate, which evaluates every British school with privately contracted inspectors during five-day visits. The inspectors study student work, school reports and finances, and report their conclusions to the school director and national educational authorities to assist in decisionmaking for each school.[15] This quantitative and qualitative information will be used to evaluate schools and will ultimately result in consequences ranging from intervention to recognition of excellence.

Time

Superintendent Payzant pointed out that one of the greatest obstacles to the success of this reform will be time. As Neil Sullivan, president of the Boston Private Industry Council, pointed out, "the pace of systemic change is often glacial." Simply getting a message to take hold in a midsized urban district like Boston takes time. Payzant suggested that the public lacks a "sense of urgency." Before his arrival, there was a sense that the state of Boston's schools was a condition rather than a problem. Payzant has attempted to change this by raising awareness of the problem through publicizing school performance.

Public education is a political matter, and politicians often cannot wait for a slowly developing reform to mature naturally. Mayor Menino has staked his political legacy on improving the schools. From his perspective the public needs to see demonstrable change before the next election or this reform effort could unravel. Superintendent Payzant appears to be committed to the long haul; he has recently committed to a second five-year contract.

Summary

Boston is at an early phase of its reform efforts, but it is in an excellent position to make major systemic reforms. It has all of the fiscal, human, and political resources in place. In three years it has made significant progress in developing complex systemwide reforms. BPS can point to standards, an accountability policy, and an innovative Whole School Change model as signs of substantial progress. The organization is focused on its core mission of improving teaching and learning. Perhaps more important, it is self-reflective and willing to adapt.

But despite these early successes Boston faces some major challenges. It needs to align its reform efforts and resources so that teachers and administrators are not overwhelmed to the point of paralysis. It must ensure that the educators in the system are well qualified, well trained, and well supervised. Recruiting and keeping good teachers and weeding out ineffective ones seems the key to addressing the district's student performance goals. Finally, time is a challenge. BPS has to balance the measured pace necessary to improve the entire system with the need to establish the credibility of this reform quickly. The current conditions for reform in Boston represent a brief window of opportunity.

MEMPHIS CITY SCHOOLS

In 1995 the Memphis City School District was chosen as one of ten "scale-up" jurisdictions for New American Schools (NAS), a research-based, whole-school designs company that offers curriculum packages for entire schools and provides assistance in putting them into practice. In the 1998–99 school year each of the district's 162 schools have signed on for one of nine whole-school design models, including six designs of the New American Schools as well as other models, including Accelerated Schools, Paideia, and Voices of Love and Freedom, making Memphis one of only eleven districts in the country to implement whole-school designs districtwide. The time line for scaling-up reflects a sense of urgency in the need to improve performance of schools throughout this high-poverty district.

The Memphis City School District reform is important not only because of the central administration's wholehearted investment in the whole-school design movement, but also because the district, before its designation as a New American Schools scale-up jurisdiction, had laid out systemic reforms aligning accountability and student testing with curriculum and instructional methods. These reforms are based on best practice, professional development, and school-level governance. For the district, the whole-school design models represent an opportunity to carry out best practice on a broad scale.

The strategic plan for school reform was developed with extensive community participation, which built political capital for the district's efforts, giving the reform strong internal as well as external support. But in carrying out the reforms, the district has experienced tension between those orchestrating the program at the district level and those who are responsible for making changes happen in the classroom.

District administrators know that if the reform programs are to continue, local leaders will need to see improved student achievement within a relatively short time. Early results from the student achievement tests are encouraging: twenty-five schools involved in the first round of implementing whole-school design models in the 1995–96 school year showed a 7.5 percent gain over students nationwide in the state's standardized test, and a 14.5 percent gain over comparable Memphis City Schools at the end of the 1997–98 school year.[16] Researchers from RAND, Johns Hopkins University, and the University of Memphis, who are studying efforts to scale-up the NAS designs, will continue to track student achievement.

Meanwhile, principals and teachers struggle with the pace and scale of change, the value of importing curriculum, and sometimes the fit between the particular whole-school design model they have chosen and their school, as well as the heavy attention the district has devoted to measuring progress through student test scores. Many question the extent to which schools in a high-poverty district with a highly mobile student population can make a difference in student achievement. Many feel the need for greater recognition and appreciation of their efforts from the district.

Case Study

This case study describes the Memphis strategy. It summarizes the key elements of the reform strategy in terms of intent and how well it is working in practice. The case study was developed through a two-part process:

—two week-long visits to Memphis by a University of Washington researcher in April 1998 and November 1998. The researcher interviewed the superintendent, administrators, union leaders, principals, teachers, parents, students, and community and business leaders.

—a review of public documents describing the city's reform plans and a variety of news reports about the progress of those plans.

The House Administration

Memphis Superintendent Gerry House came to her job in 1992, never having led a large urban district . Before her arrival in Memphis she had served as superintendent of the much smaller and more prosperous Chapel Hill–Carrboro, North Carolina, school district.[17] In Memphis she faced the pervasive challenges of poverty, high student mobility, poor student achievement, and high dropout rates.

House is described as an energetic, hands-on, methodical, and determined leader. True to this description, she approached the challenges of her new job systematically. Soon after her arrival in Memphis, she initiated a strategic planning process, gathering information and opinion from teachers, principals, parents, the Memphis City School Board, and representatives of the business community and other community members. Although House's vision for the district has clearly helped shape the strategic plan, community input was also incorporated. This participation has paid off in terms of political support for the reform effort.

The superintendent is a strong believer in the power of organizational and incentive structures to influence reform and has reorganized the central office along functional lines, creating a cabinet with three associate superintendents for the offices of Business Operations, Student Programs and Services, and School Reform, and two executive directors, one for Communications and Administrative Services and one for Research, Standards and Accountability. House describes this five-person cabinet as her "guiding coalition."

Named 1999 superintendent of the year by the American Association of School Administrators, House has also attempted to decentralize decisionmaking by limiting layers of bureaucracy in the central office. The district now has twelve "principal clusters," with cluster leaders nominated by their peers, to provide leadership and to serve as a communications link between the central office and the schools. According to the central office, each of the district's 162 principals also has direct access to the superintendent, although the number of principals puts a practical limit on the amount of attention each might be able to receive.

In addition to addressing organizational challenges, House believes that an essential part of her job has been to cause people to question their low expectations for students, develop greater awareness regarding what students will need to succeed in the twenty-first century, and help schools develop their own vision of what schools and classrooms would look like if all children were leaving school ready for careers and work. In her speeches the superintendent often invokes the image of "Promise Street," describing what the district would look like if reforms were fully implemented.

Although House has not always won the praise of principals and teachers, who feel a great deal of pressure to change at a rapid pace, there is little controversy over the goals of the reform within the district. House maintains a strong base of support for her efforts with school board members and in the community.

In 1999, six years after the adoption of the district's strategic plan, Superintendent House can point to the accomplishment of many of the goals set out in the 1993 plan. She acknowledges that the district still faces many challenges following the years of hard work she and others throughout the district have already invested.

Demographics

Memphis is the twentieth largest urban school district in the country with 162 schools serving 112,000 students. It is a high-poverty district: in the 1997–98 school year, approximately 70 percent of the students received a free or reduced-price lunch, and 101 of the district's schools received federal Title I funds for disadvantaged students.

The city school district has experienced some white flight, and the proportion of white students in the Shelby County schools, where Memphis is situated, is much higher than in Memphis city schools. Within Memphis city schools, 85 percent of students are African American, 13 percent white, and 2 percent other ethnicities.

Although Memphis city schools have never been subject to court-mandated busing orders, the district has created twenty-eight "optional schools" with magnet programs to encourage greater integration. In addition to these schools, the district experimented with reforms at some of the city's most troubled inner-city schools in the late 1980s. These schools were freed from following most district regulations, focused on site-based management principles, and built from the ground up with the site councils hand-selecting principals and teaching staff. Site councils are still active at these schools. Attendance at the district's optional schools is based on admission standards and space availability. These schools are very popular, and parents are known to camp out overnight in an attempt to increase chances of their children's attendance.

Student mobility is a significant factor in Memphis. Approximately one-third of the students change schools during the year, often more than once according to district officials. Although students may petition to remain in a school should their family move, the district does not provide transportation, and the city's public transportation system is limited.

Finances

The operating budget for Memphis city schools is funded by the city, county, state, and federal governments. In 1992 the Tennessee courts mandated that the state develop new funding formulas. That same year the state legislature responded with the Basic Education Plan, and Memphis has benefited from the new funding formulas of this legislation.

In fiscal year 1998 the district had a budget of $550 million. According to the district, approximately 80 percent of the budget goes directly to instruction, and only 2.6 percent is spent on administration (people such as the superintendent, associate superintendents, and their staffs). The remaining 17.4 percent funds personnel services, employee relations, school maintenance, transportation, security, and other operations. Teachers are paid an average salary for the southeastern United States. The school system is the second largest employer in Memphis.

In the 1996–97 school year, the most recent for which data are available, the district spent an average of $4,875 per pupil, $1,010 below the national average and $259 below average expenditures for the south-eastern states.

Resources for implementation of New American Schools and other models have been scarce. Although the local Partners in Public Education (PIPE) foundation has provided funding for many schools in the first year of carrying out a whole-school design, schools must find resources for the second- and third-year programs within their discretionary budgets, presenting challenges, in particular, to non-Title I schools.[18]

The Reform Strategy in Theory

The mission of the Memphis School District is "to prepare all children to be successful citizens and workers in the 21st century. This will include educating them to read with comprehension; write clearly; compute accurately; think; reason; and use information to solve problems."[19] To fulfill this mission, the district emphasizes the following interrelated elements that are described in greater detail later:

—accountability and development of standards for improved student achievement;

—curriculum and instructional methods with a focus on professional development and use of best practices; and

—school-level governance.

Accountability and Development of Standards

As required by Tennessee's Education Improvement Act of 1992 all students participate in an annual assessment, the Tennessee Comprehensive Assessment Program (TCAP). There are four components to the TCAP. The first is the TerraNova test, which is used to measure student achievement in reading and language arts, mathematics, science, and social studies for students in grades 3–8, and is a nationally normed test. The second component is administered to students in grades 4, 7, and 11, who must participate in the writing assessment (students are required to write an essay on a specific topic). The third component, the competency test, is a state-developed test measuring mathematics and reading and language arts skills that is administered to students in the eighth

grade. (Students who do not pass the test are given several more opportunities to take it. Under state requirements, they must pass the competency test and meet certain course requirements before they can
graduate.) The fourth component is a high school subject matter assessment for mathematics (prealgebra through algebra II, geometry, and
math for technology). Students are not required to pass the subject matter assessment tests, but the scores are one part of measuring student
achievement and a school's effectiveness.

Assessment is an important part of the district's accountability plan,
and this is perhaps the most controversial element of the reform program. The controversy centers not so much on whether principals and
teachers should be held accountable for student performance but whether
student performance should be used to evaluate the performance of principals and teachers. As of 1998 some 60 percent of each principal's performance evaluation rests on student performance on the TCAP tests.
Principals are evaluated once every three years through the district's principal performance evaluation process. Principals must be able to show
that their school's students have both met established targets and made
relative improvements on the TCAP and other achievement tests.[20] Other
components of the process include a school climate survey of parents,
faculty, and students (15 percent of the evaluation), evaluation of the
school improvement plan (10 percent), and evaluation of the principal's
portfolio (15 percent). Teachers do not face the same evaluation process
by the district, and many principals believe this is unfair. However, teachers and union representatives argue that teachers are indeed held accountable for student performance, because they are likely to receive poor
evaluations from their principals if their students do not perform well.

In addition to these concerns, many principals and teachers are skeptical about the link between the teaching methods they are being asked
to adopt and improved student performance on TCAP tests. Some argue that factors beyond their control, such as education level of the
mother, have much more to do with student achievement than anything
teachers are able to do. Others argue that achievement measures should
include more sophisticated assessments, not just performance on a single
test. (Although the district has developed a more comprehensive set of
standards, known as lifelong learning standards, district evaluation of
these measures counts for a much smaller percentage of principal performance reviews.) Many believe that if TCAP test scores are to be used

as the district's primary measure of student achievement, achievement should be based on relative improvement of students and there should be no set performance targets.

These reactions are not universal. Some principals and teachers view the TCAP test scores as yet another tool that will aid them in identifying their students' strengths and weaknesses and direct their teaching efforts to areas where students need the most help. They see the TCAP tests as being closely linked to their curriculum and believe that principals and teachers, working together, can help boost student scores. Nevertheless, it is fair to say that, in general, principals and teachers believe that the district has placed too much focus on negative incentives in an already pressure-filled environment and that there is need for greater appreciation and acknowledgement of their hard work.

Improvements in test scores will certainly help counterbalance some of the pressures felt by teachers and principals, and the early results are showing a correlation between student achievement gains and the implementation of whole-school designs. According to research by the University of Memphis, the University of Tennessee at Knoxville, and Johns Hopkins University, students in twenty-five elementary schools that had been using whole-school designs for two years showed greater improvements on state tests than did students in a control group of schools that had not yet adopted whole-school design models. Researchers will continue to monitor test results to determine whether gains hold in the long run.[21]

Curriculum and Instructional Methods

House believes that true reform happens in the classroom, and professional development for teachers and principals is a central part of her strategic vision for the Memphis City School District. The district's newly established Teaching and Learning Academy (TLA) and investment in the whole-school design movement are seen as mutually reinforcing approaches to professional development.

Plans for the academy were laid before Memphis signed on for NAS whole-school designs. Soon after her arrival in the district, House raised $2 million from the Memphis-based Partners in Public Education for a Teaching and Learning Academy to promote professional development for all district employees. The academy opened its doors in April 1996.

The academy building itself has a friendly yet businesslike atmosphere, sending a message of professionalism to teachers and principals. The TLA regularly hosts speakers of national stature, sponsors locally developed training programs, and serves as a central location for teachers and principals to meet informally. Workshops focus on effective teaching and learning, innovative leadership, and school redesign.

School-Level Governance

The principle that decisions should be made as close to the point of implementation as possible is also an important element in the district's strategic plan. The district has attempted to decentralize decisionmaking in three ways. First, it has allowed each school to choose, from a menu of options, which whole-school design best suits its own philosophy of education and style of operation. Second, it has provided schools with some fiscal flexibility through site-based budgeting. Third, the district supports participatory decisionmaking at the school level through site councils, which have been established in every school.

Choice among whole-school designs is the primary way the district has decentralized decisionmaking. Although each school is required to implement a whole-school design, there are still options among which schools can choose. Whole-school designs are intended to provide teachers and schools with the tools needed to help students meet district and state standards. Teachers and principals, however, are somewhat cautious about the whole-school designs. The designs have not previously been tested on a districtwide scale, and some feel they may not be suited for a high-poverty urban district. Researchers at RAND, Johns Hopkins University, and the University of Memphis are studying the process by which schools have chosen the particular whole-school design they are using, and how that process has affected perceptions regarding the fit and subsequent implementation of the design. Another concern is that standards established at the district and state levels were not developed with the whole-school design curricula in mind. Teachers and principals are somewhat skeptical about the ability of the designs to help them meet these standards. According to teachers and principals, the survival of the whole-school designs in Memphis will likely require a clear increase in test scores.

The district has provided schools with some fiscal autonomy through site-based budgeting. However, they have only a limited amount of discretionary funding available, and significant amounts are already earmarked for purchase of whole-school design curricula, on-site professional development, textbooks, sports equipment, band instruments, and the like. Schools whose principals and faculty are not natural entrepreneurs may not be effective in raising additional funds through grants or special fund-raising events.

The establishment of a site council in every school encourages school-level governance. However, representation is not always effective. The councils are usually composed of three parent representatives and three teacher representatives, and communication from the group to the community is often limited. In addition, the councils have only limited authority in regard to strategic decisionmaking. Councils in schools without strong leadership or a history of parent and teacher involvement do not take advantage of the opportunity to influence curriculum issues or suggest how the school's discretionary resources might most effectively be spent. Under the district's strategic plan, neither school-level leaders nor site-leadership councils have control over basic staffing decisions.

The Reform Strategy in Practice

Carrying out the reform has required careful shepherding by central office leaders and school principals to ensure that day-to-day operations translate into the larger strategic vision. The strategy of the district has involved regular communication regarding goals of the reform, reliance on strong leadership from principals, and continuous monitoring and evaluation.

Regular Communication

The district's Department of Communications and Administrative Services has developed communication plans for each of the major components of the reform, including standards development, accountability, and selection of whole-school designs. Communication plans address the purposes for each of the elements of the reform and suggest how to communicate these purposes to the district's various constituents.

There appears to be clear understanding at the school level regarding goals of the district and the role of individual schools in the district's reform effort. Where there are communication difficulties, they appear to be associated with the sheer quantity of information as well as the problem of communicating from the school level to the central office.

Schools also believe they lack time to understand the implications of various initiatives for their curriculum. This last matter presented some difficulties for schools within the first New American Schools cohort. In many cases, teachers and principals felt that they did not have a complete picture of how particular models would work in their own schools. More schools have begun to implement whole-school designs in each year since 1996. Greater experience with the designs has ameliorated some of this confusion. There is now more craft knowledge of what is entailed in signing on for each of the designs and more sharing of experience among schools.

Reliance on Strong Principal Leadership

Principals serve as a vital link between district leaders, who are responsible for orchestrating various elements of the reform, and teachers, who are responsible for carrying out the reform at the classroom level. According to House, good principals combine the qualities of a strong instructional leader with that of a dynamic school leader who can inspire teachers, reach out to parents and community leaders, and take advantage of district and community opportunities that will improve their school.[22] The district's cadre of principals includes several exemplary models of such leadership.

The district has experienced a fairly high turnover rate among its principals in the past five years. According to teachers and principals, at least some of this turnover can be attributed to the pressure principals feel to increase student performance. A few principals have been counseled out, and others have taken advantage of early retirement.

To fill vacancies, the district recruits principals across the country and has succeeded in hiring several from other areas. However, district leaders express concern regarding the national shortage of well-qualified principals, and note that they are attempting to address this shortage by nurturing local talent. The district has developed a program with the

University of Memphis for new principals and has sent at least fifty principals to Harvard's summer program for educational leadership. In addition, the district sponsors professional development programs for principals at the Teaching and Learning Academy.

Monitoring and Evaluation

House describes the Memphis reform as data driven, and the district has devoted significant time and resources to developing measures, gathering and evaluating data, and developing feedback mechanisms to help schools that are experiencing difficulty adjust their curriculum and instruction.

In addition to monitoring student achievement through the state-mandated TCAP tests, the district's Department of Research, Standards and Accountability holds responsibility for

—developing and implementing assessment tools intended to complement standardized tests,

—monitoring districtwide student outcomes,

—developing lifelong learning standards,

—developing and managing systems for reporting progress toward goals and objectives in the district's strategic plan,

—evaluating each school's improvement plan,

—assessing school climate, and

—gathering data for evaluation of school staff.

Although student performance on standardized tests is the most important measure by which the education reform efforts will be judged, the district has also developed eighteen standards for lifelong learning intended to complement the state's standardized tests. The standards were developed with ideas from stakeholders throughout the community, particularly business leaders. The district also developed performance indicators for what children should be able to do in meeting each of the standards and provided extensive training for teachers and principals in mapping of curriculum standards, developing integrated units, and finding ways in which whole-school designs can help students to meet the standards.

The availability of data allows the district to monitor effectiveness of design models and of school-level implementation. As a next step the district plans to develop clear consequences for schools that are not meeting standards.

Summary

Five years after the adoption of the strategic plan, Gerry House can point to the accomplishment of many of its goals, developed with the participation of staff, students, parents, and other community members. She enjoys a supportive board and little opposition to the reform. She was selected as 1999 superintendent of the year by the American Association of School Administrators. The district has increased accountability and professional development for all staff. Test scores of schools carrying out the whole-school designs showed a 14.5 percent gain over comparable Memphis city schools at the end of the 1997–98 school year. The greatest threat to the reform is whether test scores will rise quickly enough to maintain teacher support, an especially sensitive issue because teachers and principals express fatigue and feel underappreciated. If scores do not continue to rise, House may lose the energy and commitment of the teachers and principals that currently power the reform.

NEW YORK CITY DISTRICT 2

New York City's Community School District 2 in Manhattan is known for innovative professional development and a focus on reading. Anthony J. Alvarado, superintendent of District 2 for eleven years until 1998, made this statement his mantra: "It's about instruction, and only instruction."[23]

During Alvarado's tenure District 2 moved from the middle of the pack to the second-highest performing school district in New York City. Researchers and educators from all over the country descended on the district to learn why. One distinguishing characteristic of District 2: it focused on teaching and learning, not the many other demands of running schools. In particular, Alvarado emphasized strengthening literacy. The system worked well because there was a common mission. This reform strategy is intriguing because it is simple in design, consistent in delivery, and most important, effective.

Case Study

Because of the heavy research interest in District 2, this case study was developed through several resources.

—A visit to New York City by an East Coast researcher in March and August 1998. The researcher interviewed the superintendent and university-based researchers who have studied the district.

—An analysis of recently published studies about the district, including extensive work by the researchers at the High Performance Learning Communities Project at the University of Pittsburgh (led by principal investigators Lauren Resnick, Richard Elmore, and Anthony Alvarado) who have produced a series of articles and a video on the district.

—A review of newspaper articles and published reports.

The Alvarado Administration

Anthony Alvarado has been recognized as an educational leader who is both charismatic and controversial. Rudy Crew, New York City chancellor, described Alvarado's influence this way: "His ability to think outside the box helped shape outstanding schools and restored confidence in public education."[24] The district has inspired intensive teacher training programs, an extended school day, the establishment of standards to be met by all students, and other citywide reform initiatives. A large part of his success had to do with his long collaborations with Deputy Superintendent Elaine Fink and Director of Professional Development Beatrix Johnstone. These two women conduct the bulk of the on-site work at the schools and helped create the strategy that emerged in District 2.

Demographics

Community School District 2 is a relatively small district of elementary and middle schools in Manhattan. Its 22,000 students are distributed throughout 24 elementary schools, 7 middle schools and 17 option schools (schools organized around a particular theme and serving various grade levels).[25]

By no stretch of the imagination can District 2 be considered a typical inner-city school district serving a pocket of entrenched poverty made up almost exclusively of African American or Latino students. The district is socioeconomically and culturally diverse. It draws students from poor and wealthy neighborhoods. The proportion of students eligible for free and reduced lunches varies by school, although the average is about 50 percent. Approximately 20 percent of the students (primarily Asian and Hispanic) are limited in English proficiency, but again the proportions vary substantially by school from approximately 50 percent to 1 percent. The racial and ethnic compositions of the schools vary by neighborhood and school. Thirty-four percent of District 2's students are Asian, 29 percent white, 22 percent Latino, 14 percent African American, and less than 1 percent Native American.

The district as a whole has the second highest mathematics and reading scores in the city, but not every school is doing well. Although 80 percent of the students at Intermediate School 877 were reading at the highest quartile on the Comprehensive Test of Basic Skills (CTBS), less than 7 percent of the students at Intermediate School 070 were reading at that level.[26]

The Strategy in Theory

We examined District 2's strategies in theory—what the elements of the reform entailed—and found four main ones: defined roles and responsibilities, a focus on teaching and learning, investment in people, and choosing good principals.

Defined Roles and Responsibilities

Alvarado said he wanted to create a *system* of successful schools. This goal was directed at an often remarked problem in school reform: it is fairly easy to find isolated examples of successful schools but nearly impossible to find a successful district. Alvarado struggled to develop a district strategy that was neither so rigid that it straitjacketed individual school autonomy nor so unfocused that it trivialized the responsibilities of the district and shifted the onus of school success to the individual schools. Alvarado saw the district's responsibility as one of establishing a vision for the system, providing ample opportunities for principals and teachers to gain the training they need to meet district goals, and ensuring that good principals are in place at each school.

Alvarado conveyed the district's vision and direction through professional development offerings, district publications, and monthly principal meetings. The message was always the same. The mission of each school is about one thing and one thing only: student learning.[27]

A Focus on Teaching and Learning

To create a system of good schools, District 2 *simplified* rather than lowered its expectations. For over seven years there was a focus on literacy. Three years ago, mathematics was included. Alvarado said, "Schools are experimenting with a host of good ideas—community service, school-to-work, parent involvement. I think those things are great, but I don't ask about them, I just ask them how the kids are doing in reading." The district office explains its rationale for its unwavering focus on instruction this way: "If you start with instruction, you can work your way to community. If you go after community, you may never get to instruction."[28]

District 2 believes that all students can meet the same high standards. Therefore, the district chose the New Standards project as the district benchmark and focused all its fiscal and human resources on improving student reading and writing. The rationale for focusing on literacy was based on a number of factors.

—Literacy is the basis for all other subject area learning.

—Literacy is manageable. Referring to the pressure on elementary school teachers to be able to teach every subject well, Alvarado said in an interview at the Brookings Institution, "That poor elementary teacher is supposed to have the knowledge base of every departmental teacher of every subject in a high school. . . . It's impossible."

—Literacy takes time to take root. Focusing substantial resources on it for a long time enabled teachers to gain a deeper understanding of the content and skills necessary to teach it.

—Literacy provided a common understanding among teachers and administrators of what good student work looked like.

Investment in People

From Alvarado's perspective, what is wrong with education in America is simply that the "adults don't know what to do." He explained his rationale by describing his own teaching experience. "I thought I was a good teacher, [but] there were things I didn't know—what to do with certain kids at certain times. I knew I wasn't adding to their knowledge base. [I realized] 'it's not the kids, it's me.'" For this reason District 2 strives to be an adult learning system.

Professional development in District 2 takes many forms, such as

—the Professional Development Lab, which provides sixteen to twenty teachers the opportunity to spend three weeks with a master teacher as well as ongoing collaboration throughout the year;

—consultants and in-district staff developers who work directly with individual teachers or teams on specific instructional issues;

—intervisitations and peer networks (that involve 300 total days of professional time) permit teachers and principals to visit schools in and outside the district to share best practices;

—off-site training, which involves all staff from a given school attending the same workshops and receiving continuing classroom support following the training; and

—district oversight, which involves district visits at least twice a year.[29]

As part of the district oversight, Johnstone and Fink visit every classroom in every school and then discuss their observations, professional development options, and potential personnel changes with the principal.

Choosing Good Principals

District 2 administrators believe that the key to creating school cultures that are both focused and open to learning lies in good principals.[30] A good principal in Alvarado's eyes is a strong instructional leader first, then a good administrator. Principals are responsible for balancing the professional development needs of their individual teachers with the collective demands of their schools.[31] Finally, a good principal hires good people and knows whom to counsel to leave the system when professional development efforts have been unsuccessful. Alvarado said, "You will be judged as a principal by the staff you leave in place."[32]

Thus in theory District 2's strategy has many potential benefits. It has clear standards, a literacy focus within those standards, and compelling professional development methods to enable teachers to prepare their students to attain the standards. By focusing for an extended period on improving literacy, the strategy has helped the collective capacity of district personnel grow and, by extension, the educational experiences of the students to improve. The district's heavy reliance on its principals enables schools to be autonomous while also serving as the "connective tissue" providing a common knowledge base among schools.[33]

The Strategy in Practice

In an interview Alvarado described the day-to-day workings of the district this way:

> On some days it looks like this is a bottom-up system and some days it looks like a top-down system. If you go to the schools, it should almost look like there isn't a district. But when you go to all of the schools, there is such commonality that you know there must be a system because they all couldn't be doing this kind of work as a result of "letting a thousand flowers bloom."

This variability requires subjective judgments and complex negotiations between the district and the schools.

How does District 2 balance school autonomy with central control? The superintendent and central office staff follow four principles: know the schools and gain their respect, negotiate with principals, acknowledge that nobody is perfect; and establish a culture in which everyone is accountable.

Know the Schools and Gain their Respect

To address the specific needs of each school, the district makes an effort to know every school intimately. Beatrix Johnstone and Elaine Fink visit every school two to six times a year and know every teacher in the system. "Our theory is that the line [top district administrators] needs to know instruction in order to make competent decisions," Alvarado commented. "The leadership of an organization has to know the work of the organization."

Negotiate with Principals

The district administration knows that communication is a two-way street. Alvarado described it this way: "The central office sets the goals, but they are dynamic, there's this back and forth. . . . We communicate, negotiate, argue, and resolve. That's the way it works." Johnstone and Fink block out time for each principal to negotiate budgets (some meetings require a whole morning). By having to voice their priorities, principals are forced to clarify their school's strategy to the district office. This process helps schools actually do what they set out to do. And by encouraging principals to challenge ineffective professional development models and outdated texts, the district as a whole continually improves the services delivered to students. This willingness to question and negotiate is evident within the district office as well. In an interview Alvarado said, "It can get pretty hot over there [pointing to a table mounded with papers]. That's where Elaine, Bea, and I strategize. And we certainly don't always agree, but that's why we keep growing—we question what we're doing all the time."

Acknowledge That Nobody Is Perfect

In most schools, teachers are isolated. They shut their doors and rarely admit their problems or share their successes. To create a system of good schools, District 2 tried to break down the walls of isolation through what one researcher, Mary Stein, calls "deprivatizing."[34] This is exemplified in principals' allowing their peers to do walk-throughs of their buildings and the willingness of teachers to visit other classrooms and be visited in their own. District administrators have tried to create a culture that is built on the premise that the system can always be improved. Alvarado was quoted as saying, "The message was loud and clear and consistent: It is all right to have less-than-perfect performance: the important thing is to adopt the stance of a learner so that improvement is possible."[35] Therefore the onus is on everyone in the system to be open to critique and to be willing to share best practices.

Establish a Culture in Which Everyone Is Accountable

Alvarado suggested there were two elements to his accountability system: data and process. He and others in the central office review test scores, but they also look at what is happening at the school. Based on these data they evaluate what actions need to be taken. Alvarado said in an interview, "sticks don't inform, they just hit." Although he agrees that consequences are necessary, he also believes that firing everyone who does not meet the standard without providing the necessary coaching does not address the need to build capacity in a system.

This accountability system informs the district's human resource policy. "We are very careful about who we bring into the system. Once they're here, we monitor them closely and provide them help in areas where they need help. If teaching simply isn't their strength, we counsel them out." In fact, more than half of the teachers and principals in District 2 have turned over during Alvarado's tenure. Accountability in District 2 means being selective in the first place, monitoring closely, providing appropriate professional development once hired, and weeding out those that do not fit. Alvarado went on to say, "over time, the overall quality in the system has risen, so now we do far less weeding."

Summary

District 2 has enjoyed some noteworthy successes. A focused and sustained effort, the reform has had a decade in which to become institutionalized. Clear responsibilities at the district and school levels have been instrumental in systemic improvement. When district administrators establish a clear direction for the district, hire good principals, and monitor student progress carefully, individual principals may be freed up to determine the best means to meet the central standards. Grounded and focused professional development provides more effective support than random workshops.

Every strategy has limitations. In District 2 the ability to replicate this model appears to be its greatest limitation. This reform strategy is occurring in a small elementary and middle school district. The district is not a typical inner-city one and has benefited from the leadership of an exceptionally skilled and veteran administration. The limited age-range served is important because most urban centers face their greatest challenges when attempting to educate high school students. In addition, because this district is part of a network of districts, it can draw in new teachers and transfer out less desirable ones with relative ease. Finally, Superintendent Alvarado is a nationally recognized educator, and Johnstone and Fink appear to be exceptionally strong. Therefore the question is: "Can the components of this plan be reassembled and be equally successful in a different city?"

In the spring of 1998 Alvarado accepted the position of chancellor of instruction in the San Diego public schools, second in command under Superintendent Alan D. Bersin. The District 2 board has appointed Elaine Fink as superintendent to replace Alvarado.

THE SAN ANTONIO INDEPENDENT SCHOOL DISTRICT

The San Antonio Independent School District is known nationally for its effort to introduce comprehensive school reform through districtwide use of the New American Schools reform models. The reform is broader than that, however. It is about the struggle of introducing dramatic change in a district that had long been stagnant, trimming central office staff, focusing on instruction, and daring people to challenge themselves and take risks. At the same time, political swings, campuses overwhelmed by the rate and intensity of change, and a hasty implementation process are very real threats to institutionalizing these reforms.

San Antonio has emerged as a district to take note of, receiving national recognition for its reforms.[36] It is funded by major foundations and is being studied by research institutes and universities.[37] Whether the district can carry out and maintain the multiple initiatives remains to be seen. The sudden resignation of the superintendent in late 1998 has exacerbated these challenges, calling into question the district's ability or even intent to sustain current initiatives.

Case Study

This case study describes the theories behind the strategy of reform and the actions taken to implement it in San Antonio. The case study was developed through a two-part process:

—interviews by University of Washington education researchers. The interviews took place over two-week-long visits in 1998, once in May and once in October. People interviewed included the superintendent, administrators, union leaders, principals, teachers, parents, students, and community and business leaders.

—a review of public documents describing San Antonio's reform plans and a variety of news reports about the progress of those plans.

The Lam Administration

For years the schools in San Antonio Independent School District were considered among the poorest performers in the state. Out of its ninety-five schools, forty-five were on the probation list of the worst schools in the state in 1994 and were threatened with state-mandated reconstitution. The district was rife with low expectations and inadequate accountability systems. In 1994 school board members signaled their willingness to take a risk when they hired a superintendent with a reputation for implementing change. Diana Lam was born and raised in Peru and came to San Antonio by way of superintendencies in Dubuque, Iowa, and Chelsea, Massachusetts.

Lam was the first woman and second Hispanic to serve as superintendent in San Antonio. She took risks, moved quickly, and often had as many people fiercely opposed to her decisions as she had supporting them. Some of the opposition in San Antonio came from her failure to include all interested parties in the early planning of new initiatives. The story of her near sacking in 1995 is legendary in the region. After a year of reforms that involved scaling back the board's reach, the board planned to buy out her contract. Hearing this, Lam and her supporters worked quickly to rally people to her defense. Business and civic leaders along with parents, teachers, and other community members came to the board meeting to show their support. Her victory that night (the board abandoned its plan to buy her out) appeared to signal a turning point for her administration. Effectively, it quelled the opposition on the board and started an era of more intense reforms.

However, in early 1998 the aftershocks of additional controversial decisions turned the tide against her. Many point to her unpopular decision to reconstitute a popular high school as a major factor. Despite vocal support for her and her reforms from the business community and the local newspaper, the single-minded opposition of important voting groups combined with a low voter turnout swung the school board elections. Lam's board supporters were ousted and the pace of change slowed. It was probably just a matter of time until she followed her board supporters out the door.

Newspapers reported the growing friction between the board and Lam. At the heart of the dispute were disagreements over the various initiatives and board decisions to increase staff pay and cut taxes during a time of tight budgets. Adding to this, staff complaints about the pace of change, poor implementation practices, and what some felt were well-intentioned but unreasonable mandates caused the school board to buy out Lam's contract. The board's vision for the future of the district remains unclear.

Demographics

There are eighteen school districts in the greater San Antonio area. The San Antonio Independent School District is located in the heart of the city and serves a higher proportion of disadvantaged students than the other districts. The district had ninety-five schools and 60,679 students in the 1996–97 school year. The ethnic composition of students is 84 percent Hispanic, 10.7 percent African American, 5 percent Anglo, 0.2 percent Asian or Pacific Islander, and 0.1 percent Native American.

According to the district, 92 percent of students come from low-income homes. Sixteen percent have limited English proficiency and 11.7 percent receive special education services.

The District's Budget

The budget for the district's 1996–97 school year was $348 million:
—expenditures per pupil were $5,962.62;
—instruction accounted for $187 million;
—instruction-related services accounted for $43 million;
—pupil services were $50 million;
—administration (including debt service) was $1.9 million;

—plant maintenance was $38 million;

—data processing was $200,000; and

—ancillary services accounted for $452,000.

The Reform Strategy in Theory

Lam made it clear upon taking office that the district's reform package would focus on instruction when she made major organizational changes and sought external resources to fund improvements.

Internal Changes

To emphasize the focus on instruction, Lam renamed the assistant superintendents, calling them instructional stewards, an act that was not only symbolic but also substantive. She made each steward responsible for some aspect of the instructional program. She then eliminated many individual projects and programs to put fewer layers of bureaucracy between administrators and the schools. More important, she used money saved through administrative reorganization to fund school-based instructional guides, people selected for their knowledge about best instructional practice and their ability to work with teachers to improve classroom teaching.

Lam then convinced the school board to allocate $1 million for school improvement projects, and each school was invited to submit an improvement plan for approval. Lam funded school requests, but as she said, "They spent it on piecemeal programs, just like the ones we had gotten rid of. What I had wanted them to do was to come up with comprehensive change." Given the schools' response, she brought in the New American Schools (NAS) designs as a source of new ideas and bold initiatives. She told schools to choose one of the designs or submit their own ideas for an instruction-based comprehensive school improvement plan.

External Resources

San Antonio is one of only eleven school districts using the New American Schools designs districtwide. These designs concentrate on building consensus around a vision of high-quality education, and they provide comprehensive training and technical assistance. As of May 1998 some 70 percent of San Antonio Independent School District schools have adopted a design, most of which are NAS designs.

The implementation of the NAS designs has been followed by two additional initiatives not necessarily related to the designs but directly related to instruction. One is a direct-instruction reading program for elementary schools and the other a mathematics curriculum.

The Strategy in Practice

The strategy has a variety of elements.

The Instructional Guide Position

According to one outside observer, placing instructional guides in each school provides the best professional development the district has to offer. The guides themselves, usually chosen from the teaching corps, receive extensive professional development in cognitive coaching and mathematics and reading instruction. Once trained, they are assigned to schools where they develop curriculum and provide hands-on help in individual classrooms.

Although considered to be talented people, the guides report that they often had to prove themselves to their teaching colleagues. Principals laud the additions of the guide position, and many teachers welcome the guides' support, but some teachers worry about the guides' informal contributions to their yearly evaluations, and sometimes there is not a good match between the guide and the school. The district provides principal training for the guides at a nearby university, and several recent principal appointments have come from the guides' ranks, yet another indication of the emphasis on instruction.

New American Schools

School faculties looked forward to the designs' integrated curriculum and thorough professional development. They visited joint design presentations hosted by the district and visited schools already carrying out individual packages. Schools accepted the mandate in waves. Although some made an early selection, others hesitated, concerned that they had not yet determined their needs well enough to commit to a particular design. Still others looked elsewhere for ideas, even though the district funds only NAS designs.

Anecdotal evidence suggests that teachers and principals like and use the design's tenets. In some cases faculties have been so impressed that they plan to continue their involvement with the design even if the district drops funding.

Curriculum to Address Weaknesses in Teaching and Learning

The pressure to improve students' scores as measured by the Texas Assessment of Academic Skills, the state-mandated standardized testing program, continued in the district. Lam knew that NAS designs focus on curriculum organization and particular learning philosophies, but not necessarily on the acquisition of specific skills measured by the tests. Raising test scores meant focusing on basic skills. To that end she mandated districtwide implementation of two basic skills programs. One focused on a mathematics curriculum, built around the spiraling acquisition (repeated opportunities) of computational skills. Similarly, Lam mandated a reading and writing program that emphasized phonetic instruction. The writing program interconnects with the reading in such a way that the child learns one while also learns the other.

The implementation of these curriculums presented challenges. The rhetoric of building-based choice and school-based leadership conflicted with districtwide mandates. Teachers have been pressed for time to adequately learn about a new mandate and then systematically build its precepts into everyday teaching practice. Teachers also struggled with the problem of integrating what they learned in training about the new designs with what was sometimes perceived as conflicting training around the new basic skills curriculums. The district has struggled in developing a framework to integrate the two approaches.

Resources Focused on Teaching

The Lam administration was adept at focusing internal resources on instructional reforms. She moved central office curriculum staff to the schools, introduced New American Schools to provide school-level professional development, and channeled other forms of professional development to train staff and community members in the teaching reforms. The district has won large instructional, capacity-building, and evaluative grants and was able to convince the public to pass the largest facilities bond in Texas.

Although the district focused resources on the priorities of teaching and improving student learning, the board believed other matters had long been overlooked. These included a 10 percent across-the-board pay increase for all staff and administrators and a 4 percent property tax cut. These new expenses and loss of revenue caused the district to dip into its $60 million reserve; it withdrew $31 million for the 1998–99 school year alone. Many district observers thought these decisions were politically motivated efforts to appease district staff upset about the changes and to ax programs central to Lam's reforms, including the $6 million NAS designs.

Building Parent and Community Involvement

The San Antonio School District invested in the idea of strengthening parent and community involvement as a way to improve student learning and help schools stay focused on instruction. The district-created Parent and Community Partnerships Network coordinated town hall meetings, parenting skills courses, adult and community education classes (including preparation for the GED), conflict resolution classes, a newsletter distributed to all district residents, and a public access television version of the newsletter that airs twice a week. Individual school and district instructional leadership teams advise on how to improve student learning and achievement. They are composed of parents, students, business representatives, other community members, and district employees.

Although these activities appeared to be well organized and aimed at a broad audience, Lam did not develop a close alliance between the district and some of the traditional community leaders accustomed to being involved in decisionmaking. Powerful and well-respected community organizing groups, teachers' union leaders, and several of the most affected stakeholders complained that they often heard about new initiatives or changes through the same mechanisms as everyone else and heard about most initiatives after the fact. This alienated some traditional allies, and in some cases so eroded Lam's support that everything she proposed was fought. Some argued that these traditional relationships would have been more important to Lam in the long run than the excellent ones she forged in the business community.

Summary

San Antonio, once a stagnant, foundering district, was revitalized under Lam. The New American Schools designs, the internal reorganization and renaming of administrative positions, the creation of instructional guides, and the extended school calendar focused every school on instructional improvement. But political strife challenged progress. Disagreements between the Lam administration and various members of the school board, played out publicly through school board elections, undermined support for various innovations, including the financial support needed to pay for them.

The rate and intensity of change added to the challenge. Administrators have not yet integrated the more than twenty initiatives that range from new reading and math programs to the creation of standards in core academic subjects to a $400 million plan to improve facilities. Each initiative comes with its own mandates and training requirements. Each principal can be held accountable to various people, one who manages a NAS design, another responsible for a geographic region, and still others who focus on different content areas. The confusion extends to teachers, who must absorb the varied and sometimes conflicting expectations as they affect the classroom. Frontline administrative staff have felt overwhelmed and may have grown wary and resistant as a result.

Lam's resignation added to the confusion. Although some reforms have been well received by school staff (for example, the school designs and instructional guides), even these have not been institutionalized. The future of the San Antonio School District remains very unclear.

SAN FRANCISCO UNIFIED SCHOOL DISTRICT

School reform in San Francisco has been based on reconstitution, the ultimate intervention. A result of a court-ordered consent decree in 1982 in response to a suit alleging de facto segregation, reconstitution was part of a comprehensive desegregation effort to improve student achievement in impoverished neighborhoods through careful planning and infusion of additional funds. Superintendent Waldemar Rojas continued with this practice and added a system of monitoring based on data that helped identify schools in need of assistance or reconstitution.

Schools are supported by a generously funded professional development program, focused budget priorities, and an extensive database that measures the results. Schools that demonstrate their ability to educate all students retain their autonomy. Schools that do not are targeted for reconstitution, a process dreaded by principals and teachers. Many schools have been reconstituted, though the first ones received the most planning and attention and, not surprisingly, were the most successful.

The district now faces the dilemma of what to do with reconstituted schools that are not successful. In addition, a group of minority parents sued the district in 1998 to end ethnic quotas that require their children to be bused to schools outside their neighborhoods. The trial was heard by the judge who ordered the initial consent decree, and in April 1999 he found that the district has been successful at ending segregation. The district now stands to lose a significant portion of funds allotted for complying with the consent decree. And in May 1999, after seven years as superintendent, Waldemar Rojas announced that he had accepted the superintendency of the Dallas public schools.

Case Study

This case study describes the San Francisco school reform strategy. After summarizing the historical context, it highlights the most important elements of the reform strategy in terms of the intent of the reform strategy and how well it works in practice.

The case study was developed through a two-part process.

—Two three-day visits to San Francisco by a University of Washington researcher in February 1998 and November 1998. People interviewed included school administrators, union leaders, principals, teachers, parents, students, and community and business leaders. (Numerous attempts were made to speak with the superintendent, but no meeting or phone call took place.)

—A review of public documents describing San Francisco's reform plans and a variety of news reports about the progress of those plans.

The Rojas Administation

Waldemar Rojas came to the district in 1992. A controversial figure, he was viewed as a strategist and someone who could make things happen, and he enjoyed the general support of the San Francisco School Board. He was named 1998 superintendent of the year by the Association of California School Administrators. But many teachers were not enthusiastic supporters. Their antagonism heightened during contract negotiations in the spring of 1998 when Rojas received a 20 percent salary increase from the school board "for raising student test scores," while the board offered teachers no more than 5 percent. Teachers also think that Rojas sent a mixed message about shared decisionmaking (principals sharing decisions with teachers), supporting the concept more with rhetoric than action.

Demographics

In San Francisco 116 schools serve 61,054 students. The district may be one of the most diverse in the nation: Chinese make up 28.4 percent of the student body; Latinos 21.3 percent; African Americans, 16.0 percent; whites, 12.1 percent; Filipinos, 7.2 percent; Koreans, 1.0 percent; Japanese, 1.0 percent; American Indian, 0.7 percent; and other nonwhite, 12.3 percent.

Minorities make up only 45 percent of the district's 5,360 certified teachers, 2,698 of them classroom teachers. To fulfill a court order that supersedes California's initiative to end affirmative action, the district's Human Resources Department strives to make the teaching corps look more like the student body. As of September 1, 1998, 52 percent of the certificated new hires were minorities.

Finances

The district budget for the 1998–99 school year was about $521 million. The state government supplied 44 percent, the city and county governments 49 percent, and the federal government 7 percent. The average revenue per student was $7,806. The average expenditure per student was $5,378 (a figure that excluded capital improvements, maintenance, and utilities). The state funded the district at $3,836 for each K–12 student; the difference between state funding per student and the district's average expenditure was largely a result of locally funded special programs—for example, some portions of the special education program and preschool programs. Administrative overhead cost is usually figured at 7 percent of the budget.[38]

Historical Context

In June 1978 the National Association for the Advancement of Colored People (NAACP) sued the district in federal court alleging de facto segregation. The case never went to court, but the judge called both sides together to prepare a district improvement plan. He issued the 1982 consent decree that ordered the district to focus on desegregating its schools and setting up model schools to improve academic achievement. The judge further ordered that the state make a yearly contribution of $32 million to the district to enable it to act on the decree, with the district required to contribute another $8 million annually. (The NAACP also contributes a small sum each year.)

To achieve desegregation, the decree mandated that no more than 40 percent of any ethnic group could be enrolled in any one district school, a mandate that resulted in forced busing. The decree also directed the district to hire staff whose ethnic heritages mirrored those of their students. To improve academic achievement through model schools, the district selected six schools in an impoverished neighborhood and provided them with seven specific guidelines for school planning:

—removing faculty and staff and hiring new faculty and staff committed to the consent decree vision, philosophical tenets, and program;

—implementing the philosophic tenets throughout the school program;

—establishing specific "student outcomes" for each subject and grade level;

—using technology in the classroom;

—reducing adult-student ratios;

—introducing extensive staff development; and

—having new staff select a unique instructional focus for their schools.

The six schools had one year to plan, a year supported by within-district and external expertise and technical assistance as needed. At the end of the year all staff members had to reapply for their positions. Those who did not want to carry out the resulting plan or who were not reselected for their former positions transferred to open positions in other district schools; the new plans and the movement of staff essentially "reconstituted" the schools. The six schools implemented their plans in the 1983–84 school year.

The strategy was not to reconstitute large numbers of schools, but rather to underscore the possibility of reconstituting underachieving schools. The first six schools targeted became known as phase I. Three subsequent phases added sixteen schools to the project. However, according to an assistant superintendent interviewed in 1998, none of the additional schools received the support given to the six phase I schools: "Mostly we just threw money at them." During the fifth and final phase, two additional schools were targeted for improvement. The district chose only to remove staff members and hire new people and did not carry out any of the other guidelines for school planning.

The court asked a panel of experts to evaluate consent decree results. The report was issued in 1992 and concluded that, on average, students in phase I schools scored higher than their counterparts in other district schools. The schools in phases II to V did not achieve the same result. In response the court declared properly implemented reconstitution a success and specifically ordered that any of the sixteen schools in phases II through V that were not showing improved student scores should be candidates for reconstitution. The court also required that all reconstituted schools adopt the original seven-point plan in its entirety and that the district should further reconstitute at least three schools a year until the achievement scores of Hispanic and African American students were equal to those of the majority counterparts. As of May 1998 the consent decree was no longer in effect.

The Reform Strategy in Theory

The school district's focus on academic achievement stems from the long-standing challenge to educate all students, an implicit, if not explicit, acknowledgment of the system's failure to educate too many of its minority children. Superintendent Rojas built on the foundation of a well-thought-out school improvement process by developing an extensive database that affects every school in the district and by ordering each school to follow transparent accountability guidelines. The underlying philosophy assumes that schools can help every student.

School Data

In the words of many staff members, "we are a data-driven district." Each school is expected to collect and use data to build its school improvement plan. Data fall into two main categories:

—quantitative, which includes standardized testing results, graduation rates, suspensions, and the racial and ethnic makeup of the school; and

—qualitative, which includes the extent to which the school makes use of its data, parent participation, professional development, school safety, early childhood standards, service learning, and interagency collaborations.

A school is then measured by the district on its ability to reach districtwide common expectations in these categories. A school might score only 19 percent in the quantitative category, but 94 percent in the qualitative one. Schools also track class size and data on number and credentials of teachers. All these data are publicly available on the district's web page and are used by the district to determine action toward the school.

School Accountability

The district monitors the data on every school. According to one administrator, "The top performers we ignore, no change required. The middle group we reinforce and encourage. Those in trouble get help and resources." Help comes through the Comprehensive School Improvement Program or CSIP. A CSIP school has one year to improve. Asked what it meant to be placed in CSIP, a principal replied, "The district provides consultants. The school goes to the top of every list for help. You receive TLC from the downtown administration. You get more resources and attention from facilities." Another principal reported, "Everything except the walls of the schools can be changed and even then there may be renovations to the physical plant. . . . It's a systemic effort." There is no change in the school's basic funding pattern in the CSIP.

At the end of the year a team of top administrators visits the school to judge progress. The team examines the school's data and looks for evidence of an aggressive improvement plan. Failure to show improvement may lead to reconstitution. At its simplest level this means the staff is replaced. Sometimes the administration is replaced and the rest of the staff left intact for one year. At the end of that year, if no progress is evident, the teaching staff and support staff are also removed. In one instance the district removed half the staff. By the spring of 1998 twenty-four schools had been placed in the CSIP, twelve had graduated before reconstitution, and ten had been reconstituted.

The Reform Strategy in Practice

The rhetoric of a data-based process to ensure school improvement is matched by administrative support through leadership, school accountability, and school support.

Strategic Leadership

The district developed a strategic improvement plan with five goals to guide all schools:
 —improve teaching and learning;
 —include parents and the community in the educational process;
 —maintain safe learning environments;
 —provide equal access to integrated programs and activities, and
 —expand early childhood education.

Each school has some latitude in how it achieves the goals. Teachers have access to the results of the collected information, including student achievement by grade level, and they help to interpret the data. The district requires each school to develop an improvement plan based on their data and to update it annually. All schools are then put on what Rojas called, "The Red Path," a one-hundred-point system for tracking school progress.

School Accountability

Currently, school progress is judged through eight weighted indicators: trends in student achievement over a four-year period (which carries 40 percent of the weight), state assessment writing samples, school-specific alternative assessments, attendance, suspensions, grades, dropout rates, and students' requests for transfers to and from schools. Success is defined as when an entire school achieves 45 percent to 55 percent on standardized tests, once scores are aggregated and disaggregated by each ethnic group.

School Support

According to a budget administrator, the district's second funding priority (after meeting contract obligations) focused on the first two of the superintendent's yearly priorities: in 1998 it was a seventh period of instruction for grades 6 through 9, and class size reduction in grades K–3. To achieve this, each school's discretionary budget included an allotment of $19.60 for each elementary student; $27.60 for each middle school student, and $35.60 for each high school student. Schools also had discretionary use of federal and state funds provided for special populations—for example, the Title I and Limited English Proficiency programs—as long as parents and staff were included in the decisions and the dollars were spent on the children who generated them. CSIP schools received additional funds from the $40 million generated by the consent decree.

Further support comes from the Human Resources Department spurred by the need to fill positions created by the smaller class size and the court's mandate to make the teaching corps reflect the racial and ethnic mix of the student body. The district acts aggressively by offering certification classes for uncredentialed new hires and a teacher training program for the district's paraprofessionals. Currently, 80 percent of the trainees are ethnic minorities. Dollars provided by the consent decree fund recruiting trips.

The department has also established central screening of potential hires. The central office screens candidates' credentials and conducts a forty-five-minute interview that judges candidates' ability to work with urban populations. (Applicants take the state's required "trade craft" test for teachers elsewhere.) Schools interview screened candidates and make requests. For teacher candidates, the Department of Human Resources reviews the schools' choices for appropriateness. For candidates for principal, the superintendent makes the final selection. According to a human resources administrator, "The competition for minority candidates is tremendous, but being Chinese isn't enough. A candidate must demonstrate the ability to work with urban children." Only those who pass the screening are eligible for employment.

The extent of autonomy in filling professional development needs creates a challenge for a department that must also support the development of school plans, the adoption of new textbooks, and still provide specific help to CSIP schools. Professional development efforts appear as an eclectic menu of possibilities designed to provide multiple access points for school staff charged with responsibility for their own improvement. Hands-on professional development support in schools comes from expert classroom teachers assigned to work in specific schools for eight to twenty-four hours a week. Their major tasks are to provide help with the new language arts curriculum, carry information between the central office and the schools, share effective teaching strategies, interpret evaluation data, help schools develop portfolios to demonstrate their progress on The Red Path, and act as consultants in their areas of expertise. It is reported that Rojas paid for professional development by taking "2 percent to 5 percent off the top of the district's budget each year" as well as using grant funding.

Conclusion

The strengths of school reform in San Francisco include the clarity and single-mindedness of the school improvement goal, accompanied by a clear process and time line for achieving it. As one community member said, "It is not arbitrary, and it carries a reasonable time frame for improvement." The goal enjoys unified support from the school board, the superintendent, and top administrators. The teaching corps is familiar with the intent and the process, and the reform is clearly focused on the school. Although the district administration sponsors multiple initiatives, the school decides when, how, or even whether to use the various opportunities. The collected data, clearly organized and widely available, tell the story of success or failure. Struggling schools get more than identified; they get specific help, a chance to turn themselves around and succeed. Struggling staff members also get a chance for a fresh start elsewhere. Alternatively, the process can flag the need for termination, which would be by contract agreement and an entirely separate proceeding.

The district faces challenges, however, from the viewpoint of the school, the body held most accountable for the success of reform efforts. Concern is focused on planning, professional development, and administrative support.

Planning

In the words of a principal from a former CSIP school, "We put together a plan and really worked hard at it. Now we face a turnover of one-third of our staff." This principal, in a middle school with falling test scores, faced the challenge of orienting eighteen new teachers to a school plan the new teachers had no part in developing. Further staff turmoil comes from teachers who leave classrooms for additional training; one middle school had sixteen teachers out in one day. As one administrator said, "If you talked about it differently, you could say that you open a new school, give it six weeks' lead time, choose a new principal and faculty with three-fourths of the teachers in their first year and three-fourths of the teachers without credentials. It doesn't sound so attractive." Combined with that is the "onerous, ugly, demeaning process of reassigning teachers who are sent like cattle to a holding area. Principals then come down with positions for the teachers to choose."

Staff also talked about the effect of changing dollar allocations. Graduation from CSIP means the loss of CSIP funding, the very dollars used to buy the requests that helped them graduate in the first place. In another case a district-initiated budget reduction meant that a second, non-CSIP school faced the loss of a model program that brought recognition beyond the district and even the state. This was a school that had already moved its students from a rank position of 43 out of 80 schools to a rank position of 20. Success brought punishment rather than reward.

Professional Development

Schools faced with making African American and Latino test scores compare favorably with those of students from other ethnic groups report the need for different or more extensive help from professional development. For example, one middle school principal called attention to secondary teachers' lack of training in teaching older students how to read and write and do basic mathematics. "We don't currently have what we need, and there are many schools that feel the same way, and we keep asking. We think if we ask enough, they will have to respond." Some principals want to be put in touch with the research on best practices. Others want site visitations with critical feedback from knowledgeable professionals.

Coordination of professional development is a continual challenge. For example, one trainer reported that in the middle of a several-day training session for one department, an administrator from another department came into the room and pulled a substantial number of "students" out of the session to attend a second training held elsewhere. The "students" returned to the initial session for its last day. Though an administrator indicated that the district "could not get a handle on the specific amount spent on professional development," a 1995 article in *Education Week* reported an $18 million expenditure on professional development activities each year.[39] The district received a Rockefeller grant intended to help them focus the department, enlarging on successful programs and discarding others. A policy analyst said, "We're looking not so much at programs, but more at how the system for delivery is working or not. We have a lot of strong national models here, and one of the things we're finding is that it's overwhelming for a lot of people, how much is going on." In spite of the multiple offerings, some schools buy professional help from various vendors.

Administrative Support

Asked about district support, one principal replied, "The main thing they could do is leave us alone. When there is a paid staff day, let us take it to work on what we need in the building. Don't use it for district needs." However, a second principal said, "The district needs to do more hands-on stuff and not leave so much for the school to figure out. Before they leave schools to their own devices, they need to inform schools about what they expect."

Response to new hiring practices varied; some principals reported that initial screening produced the best crop of teacher candidates to date, while others could not hire valued people who failed the test. Added to this is the struggle to find credentialed candidates, a struggle exacerbated by the mandate to shrink primary and ninth-grade class size. Interestingly, standards for hiring had evidently not yet extended to paraprofessionals. One principal reported the program impact of a bilingual aide who could not speak English well enough to be understood.

Administrative Organization

In contrast to the visible planning and evaluation of schools, a specific process for improving administrative departments or evaluating the effectiveness of their services to schools is less apparent. Neither is integrated service delivery to schools across departments readily apparent. According to one administrator, "An issue we constantly address is the attitude of central and how to get resources that may not be available to a single department. We need to go east and west and not just north and south." Rojas himself said in a public forum that he had not been able to penetrate his own bureaucracy.

There also seem to be no prioritized criteria for spending the $40 million generated by the consent decree; nothing that would rationalize or prioritize how the dollars are spent other than by the guidance of the consent decree, the superintendent's priorities on the front end and the analysis of student achievement on the back end. In essence, no criteria exist for choosing between two grant requests of equal merit.

Evaluations used to judge schools draw their share of concern. Conflicting test score reports undermine confidence, as when the state makes a report that includes specific sets of students and the district report differs because it excludes those same students. Furthermore, the practice of using data to measure the success of schools is not necessarily reliable unless they measure the same students. A changing student body constantly challenges the reliability of the database. Adding to this is the suspicion that new superintendents change district tests (as Rojas did) because a changed test allows a lower baseline from which to measure progress. Although attention is given to students' social needs, only cognitive success is extensively tracked, measured, and compared.

Some of those interviewed voiced another concern. As one said, "It feels like the schools that get reconstituted are not always the worst. Sometimes it is not exactly clear how the choice about which schools get reconstituted gets made. It's like a black box. They [school staff] think it's the superintendent." When a school perceived as the worst gets more time to improve while a school perceived to be better gets reconstituted, it undermines the integrity of the entire process. (Given the objectivity of the rest of the process, a member of the administration describes the decision to reconstitute as a subjective decision based on the administration's considerable professional experience.)

Political Issues

Schooling in urban settings is aptly described as political. In San Francisco, parents of students in schools where the district pulls funds, programs, or teachers, complain regularly. School boards pass controversial policies—for example, a policy intended to micromanage high school reading lists. Contract negotiations reveal flash points of contention such as a disagreement over Rojas's decision to turn over an elementary school to the private for-profit Edison project. And the reconstitution of schools adds to the mix. One person called it "the Clint Eastwood approach to reforming schools." The panel of experts ordered by the court to study the effect of reconstitution in the consent decree said, "Your benefits don't come until three or four years down the road, but the costs are immediate. . . . What seems like a simple idea turns out, when you do it, to be a lot more complicated."[40]

Three assumptions seem to underlie San Francisco's school reform strategy. First, it is assumed that the measures chosen actually represent success or failure, that the numbers demonstrate real progress that can be sustained. Second, the district assumes that faculties presented with sets of data will respond, that they will know or have the time to figure out how to move forward. Third is an assumption that community can be built among economically, racially, and ethnically disparate groups of people and that this will lead to improved student learning. Some administrators consider teachers' attitudes and expectations the barriers to success: "We have to recruit teachers who believe that kids can learn." Others call attention to teachers' need to trust each other and the administration. Further, the consent decree directs the district to hire staff whose ethnic heritages mirror those of their students. Underlying these suggestions and the decree are the notions that successful student achievement depends on teachers, and that teachers should have good attitudes and expectations and look like the students they teach—admirable and desirable qualities, but are they the required conditions for success?

SEATTLE SCHOOL DISTRICT

In February 1999 the Seattle School Board officially appointed acting Superintendent Joseph Olchefske to the district superintendency. Olchefske, who was originally hired as the district's chief financial officer, promised to carry on the reform efforts of his predecessor and mentor, John Stanford. Stanford died in November 1998 following an eight-month battle with leukemia. During his three years as superintendent, Stanford had launched a number of reform initiatives and had, by virtue of his energy and charismatic leadership, created new commitment to school change in a lackluster district. Olchefske faces the dual challenges of following in the widely admired Stanford's footsteps as the district's spokesperson and guiding a district still in the early stages of addressing systemic reform.

Case Study

This case study describes the ideas behind the strategy of reform and the actions under way in Seattle. The case study was developed through a two-part process:

—interviews by Seattle-based education researchers in February and August 1998. People interviewed included the superintendent, administrators, union leaders, principals, teachers, parents, students, and community and business leaders.

—a review of public documents describing Seattle's reform plans and a variety of news reports about the progress of those plans.

Transition of Leadership

With the appointment of Olchefske to the superintendency, the Seattle School Board has for the second time in a row placed a noneducator at the district's helm. This action reflects the belief of several board members that colleges of education and experience in the education system do not, in and of themselves, produce individuals with the vision and leadership qualities necessary to pilot schools through successful reform efforts. John Stanford, a former major-general of the army and, at the time of his hiring in 1995, a successful county executive in Fulton County, Georgia, succeeded in fulfilling the board's expectations. Stanford significantly raised the profile of the district in the community (and the country) and launched a number of broad reform initiatives.

The reforms Olchefske has vowed to see through are very much a product of Stanford's leadership style. Although Olchefske, as a member of Stanford's cabinet, has some interest in these initiatives, he is a very different kind of leader than Stanford was and faces a number of challenges in carrying on Stanford's legacy. Stanford set out a framework for school reform, articulating a strategy of top-down policy development and bottom-up planning and implementation (described later).

However, Stanford was also known as an idea-a-minute manager who preferred to make many of his own decisions rather than delegating to staff. Staff members often had a hard time carrying through with Stanford's many proposals. In addition, the central administration decisionmaking structure diminished over the last two years of his administration, as half a dozen key positions turned over or were left vacant, including the position of chief academic officer, which was recently filled after being left open for two years. Olchefske's challenge, if he indeed carries on with Stanford's reform efforts, will be to define these initiatives, bring change to the classroom, and fill Stanford's shoes as champion of Seattle's schools.

Demographics

Of the 47,457 students enrolled in the Seattle School District's ninety-seven schools in the 1997–98 school year, approximately 41 percent were white, 25 percent Asian American, 23 percent African American, 8 per-

cent Hispanic, and 3 percent Native American. Thirteen percent of Seattle students speak one of eighty-eight different languages as their first
language. About half of the district's students receive free or reduced-
price lunches. Seattle's neighborhoods are generally segregated, with more
poor and minority families living in the south end of the city. Schools in
the north end have a reputation for being able to attract more senior
teachers and for better fund-raising abilities.

Finances

The Seattle School District's 1997–98 general fund budget was $345
million.

Of this amount,

—$202 million, or nearly 59 percent of the budget, was directed to
instruction;

—$31 million, or 9 percent of the budget, was directed to instruc-
tional support services such as guidance counseling, health, and other
services;

—$90 million, or 26 percent, was directed to school support services,
including transportation, food services, utilities, and building maintenance; and

—$22 million, or 6 percent, was directed to central administration
support.

District spending per pupil is close to average district expenditures
nationally. In 1994–95, the most recent year for which comparable data
are available, the district spent approximately $7,300 per pupil, about
$137 above the national average.

The Reform Strategy in Theory

The district's written strategic plan communicates only a small part of
the activity under way, largely because the reform program was an itera-
tive, dynamic process. Stanford's strategy was based on decentralization
through top-down policy development and bottom-up planning and
implementation, with an emphasis on increasing academic achievement,
particularly for minority students, whose test scores have for years lagged
behind those of their peers.

Standards are developed at the state and district level. The state's 1993 Education Reform Act sets academic standards for students. The Seattle School District implements these and other requirements that it has selected. Students in fifth, eighth, and eleventh grades are required to meet several district academic standards before they are promoted to the next grade, formally ending the concept of social promotion. Olchefske recently undid this policy, stating that all grades were responsible for educating students and that it was impractical to hold students back only at the fifth, eighth, and eleventh. Summer school classes are offered to those not meeting the standard.

Although the district has established a framework for school improvement, schools now have more opportunities to decide how they will help students meet state and district standards and can either develop their own curricular innovations or adopt one of several externally developed curriculum programs. Schools, however, must find the funds to pay for any expenses associated with curriculum programs or, for that matter, for any other capacity-building effort, such as teachers' professional development, within their own budgets (the Stanford administration introduced site-based budgeting to schools, providing them with greater discretion as to how they will allocate funds).

The Strategy in Practice

The district's top-down/bottom-up approach includes incentives, capacity-building initiatives, and new opportunities for school-level decisionmaking. Initiatives launched under the Stanford administration included:

—redefining the role of principal as the CEO of the school;

—reassignment of principals to match experience and skills with more or less challenging schools;

—designation of focus schools;

—a new student assignment plan to achieve voluntary integration of schools;

—a move toward site-based budgeting with funds allocated through a weighted student formula directing resources to disadvantaged students; and

—a new teacher contract establishing a trust agreement between the district and teachers and ending teacher seniority transfer.

The Principal as CEO

Stanford envisioned principals as CEOs of their schools, and one of his first actions as superintendent was to initiate a principal leadership training program. The $100,000-a-year program provided training for all principals in the district, with twelve half-day sessions addressing such subjects as accountability, staff selection and development, and instruction and development of vision and purpose within schools. Principals' reactions to the training have been mixed. Some comment that they have found the training informative and useful, and they refer to their training manuals. Some principals, however, have been offended that the central office assumed principals knew nothing about business, while others believe that the comparison of school leadership to business leadership is spurious. Still others have found that the training has not prepared them for increased responsibilities in using school-based budgeting mechanics and resolving personnel issues.[41]

The Stanford administration also initiated monthly meetings for principals to share ideas and experiences, and the district now has five coordinators at central administration offices who work directly with principals, providing reactions on performance, school plans, and other issues.

Reassignment of Principals

During Stanford's three-year tenure, fifty-two of Seattle's ninety-seven schools were assigned new principals. The shuffle has included replacement of principals who are retiring or moving from the district and reassignment of principals. Poorly performing principals have been given one last chance at a good school or reassigned to district headquarters, and high-performing principals have been brought in to improve failing schools. The district does not publicize the reasons for each principal's reassignment, but parents and teachers bemoan the loss of a well-respected principal or the coming of a principal with a bad reputation. Teachers and parents have not been included in decisions about principal assignments, an approach at odds with other portions of the district's strategy to allow schools to choose colleagues on the basis of compatibility and to build school teams. The Seattle strategy recognizes that strong leadership from principals is essential to school reform and to decentralization, but like other areas of the country, the district is struggling with a shortage of qualified principal applicants. A number of principals in the district are nearing retirement, raising additional concerns about recruiting and attracting high-quality people.

Designation of Focus Schools

In 1995 the district assigned a committee of administrators, principals, and teachers the task of monitoring schools with consistently low student achievement scores, poor school environment, and discipline and attendance problems. There were twenty-four focus schools in the district, all of them with a high percentage of disadvantaged students. These schools received extra help in the form of a small pot of money (an average of $14,000 per school) and were given priority for central office assistance with curriculum and teacher training. Principals in several of the focus schools were reassigned. If schools did not show signs of significant improvement after three years, they faced reconstitution. Two-and-a-half years into this program, the district ended the focus schools designation, explaining that it was bad for morale at the schools. The district announced that it would continue to provide assistance and monitoring, but not in such a public manner. Focus schools were shown signs of improvement, however: sixteen of the elementary focus schools were among the top thirty-three of the district's elementary schools with the most improved scores in 1997–98.

Student Assignment Plan

In November 1996 the Seattle School Board voted to end the district's eight-year student assignment plan (controlled choice) for elementary school students effectively ending mandatory busing.[42] In the place of mandatory busing the district has developed a new student assignment plan intended to promote several goals, including a return to neighborhood schools, increased voluntary integration, and incentives for schools to improve quality as they work to ensure that they are the schools of choice. Under the plan, which was phased in over the 1997–98 and 1998–99 school years, students are guaranteed a spot in their neighborhood cluster (the district has defined nine geographic clusters).

The new student assignment plan also serves as an incentive for improved school performance, because school choice injects an element of competitiveness among schools hoping to attract students to their programs. As schools adopt different school design packages, parents and students will be presented with a variety of options in the school market. However, for school choice to work well, parents and students will need to have good information as to what various schools are able to offer, their reputations for teaching excellence, and student outcomes. The district may have to perform a very difficult balancing act as it attempts to help poorly performing schools improve while also having a duty to inform parents of school performance as they attempt to choose appropriate schools. It will also need to evaluate which schools are consistently parents' last choices and be willing to radically alter or close them.

Site-Based Budgeting

Early in his administration Stanford initiated site-based budgeting, beginning an emphasis on greater school autonomy in allocating resources. Because the site-based budgeting started with an overall reduction in school budgets, school budget teams were faced with difficult choices, such as whether to lay off staff. Salaries are the bulk of the budget, and without a significant increase in freedom of funds at each school, there is little room to be very creative, particularly for schools not receiving federal Title I dollars.

Many principals believe that their budget teams are getting up to speed and have asked the district to phase in increased responsibility for school budgets. In 1997 the district introduced a pilot budgeting program to help schools make decisions as to how to spend their money most effectively. The Internet-based budget builder allows schools to create their budgets on the web, sharing ideas with other schools and working from a basic budgeting program. The tool is unique not only in its potential for providing principals with greater information and creativity regarding how they would expend resources at their schools, but also because it made school-level, line-item expenditures available to the general public for the first time, increasing school accountability.

A volunteer group of principals participated in the first year of the project. Problems such as getting computer equipment to each school, wiring the schools for the Internet, and dealing with the disparity of technological competency among principals proved to be hurdles. There has also been no formal district evaluation to measure the impact of this program (which to this point has been a free service to the district, but which the district is now bringing into its operations).

Equitable Allocation of Resources

During the 1997–98 school year the school district began a weighted student formula as a method of providing more equitable allocation of resources to schools. The weighted formula builds on the strategy developed by the previous administration, assigning more precise weights to a variety of risk categories and establishing a basic level of support for each school. However, the district has limited the areas in which schools have budgetary discretion and has made cutbacks to address funding shortfalls, so there are few resources available for innovative programs or to work toward the district's goal of closing the achievement gap between minority and white students. A few schools have received significant additional funds, but the federal Title I program continues to provide the greatest source of additional funds for schools with large numbers of disadvantaged students.

The weighted student formula generated some controversy during its development, with people expressing concerns that schools in the north end would not receive sufficient funding because they were not likely to have as many disadvantaged students. Under the compromise that was developed, schools receive a set amount for basic functions. Amounts above this are allocated on the basis of weighted considerations associated with weaker student achievement, including poverty, single-parent families, limited English proficiency, learning disability, and student achievement test scores in the lowest three deciles. Weights are also assigned for grade-level designation, greater weight being assigned to high school students.

Teacher Contracts

Leaders of the local teachers' union (the Seattle Education Association, or SEA) have been an active part of school reform efforts and have urged teachers to take risks in the name of change and "new unionism." In the spring of 1997 the SEA and the school district signed a teacher contract with two unique features: an end to transfer on the basis of seniority and the development of a trust agreement. This landmark contract was the product of a powerful, respectful working relationship between SEA executive director Roger Erskine and John Stanford.

Under the trust agreement, schools may now make their own hiring decisions. Before the agreement, hiring decisions were based on teacher seniority (principals and teachers had no say whether a senior teacher would be an appropriate fit for their school). There has been some resistance to the agreement from both teachers and principals, but most people who care about the staff and the working environment at their school are pleased that they now at least have the hiring rule book on their side to back up their decisions. In the past, principals would have to break rules or "creatively" open positions at odd times in the year to recruit a teacher they wanted to join their staff or to prevent teachers with bad reputations from choosing to work at their school.

The trust agreement is an effort to change the climate and culture of district schools, and in the eyes of leadership, sets the stage for shared responsibility and accountability between staff and administration. It gives teachers great latitude in working with the principal to set working conditions and to take instructional initiative. It was developed with much participation by John Stanford, who believed that the relationship and culture changes taking place at the district administrative levels must also take place at the school level. District and union leaders believe that all the stakeholders are involved in relationships with each other, and if they trust that disputes are not going to get out of the family and into the harsh spotlight of the media, people will be more apt to come to agreement and work out difficult issues, beginning to sow the seeds of accountability. The trust agreement also places greater emphasis on support for teachers and teacher self-evaluation, and the evaluation process is less punitive than in previous contracts.

Summary

Perhaps the most fundamental change in the Seattle School District since 1995 has been the renewed sense of optimism and excitement generated under John Stanford. His charismatic leadership won favorable attention to the district from the media, business leaders, and the community. Stanford made his mark as a leader, but his initiatives have yet to be institutionalized. That will require further development of the reform strategy, additional support and training for the implementers, and evaluation and assessment to understand where reforms are most effective and where they need to be adjusted to meet intended goals.

Notes

Preface

1. Paul T. Hill and Mary Beth Celio, *Fixing Urban Schools* (Brookings, 1998).

2. Frederick M. Hess, *Spinning Wheels: The Politics of Urban School Reform* (Brookings, 1999).

3. Anthony S. Bryk and others, *Improving School-Community Connections: Ideas for Moving toward a System of Community Schools* (Baltimore: Annie E. Casey Foundation, 1999).

Introduction

1. See, for example, Michael Harrington, *The Other America: Poverty in the United States, with a New Introduction* (Macmillan, 1964).

2. U.S. Bureau of the Census, *Current Population Reports: Education Supplement, Social and Economic Characteristics of Schools* (October 18, 1998), table 5, pp. 102–08.

3. See Douglas J. Besharov, ed., *America's Disconnected Youth: Toward a Preventive Strategy* (Washington: Child Welfare League of America, 1999), especially chapter 6, "The Hallwalkers," by Hilliard Pouncy, pp. 151–84.

Chapter One

1. The chancellor's job in New York City resembles more that of a state superintendent of instruction than that of the typical school superintendent. More ceremonial than hands-on, the chancellor's duties include budget development and presentation and public representation. The real administrative authority in New York's schools lies in the hands of thirteen district superintendents.

2. This book does not explore all the possible causes of these unfortunate facts. For a searching and constructive analysis see Christopher Jencks and Meredith Phillips, eds., *The Black-White Test Score Gap* (Brookings, 1998).

3. See, for example, L. Scott Miller, *An American Imperative: Accelerating Minority Educational Advancement* (Yale University Press, 1995).

4. National Center for Children in Poverty, "Young Children in Poverty Factsheet" (Columbia University, 1999).

5. For a thorough discussion of teacher background and competence in the inner city, see Linda Darling-Hammond, *What Matters Most: Teaching for America's Future* (New York: Teachers College Press, 1996).

6. On "effective schools" research and methods see Lawrence W. Lezotte and Beverly A. Bancroft, "Growing Use of Effective Schools Model for School Improvement," *Educational Leadership*, vol. 42 (March 1985), pp. 23–27.

7. Frederick M. Hess, *Spinning Wheels: The Politics of Urban School Reform* (Brookings, 1999), p. 5.

8. Hess, *Spinning Wheels*, pp. 3–4.

9. See Paul T. Hill and Mary Beth Celio, *Fixing Urban Schools* (Brookings, 1998), for a more complete description of each of the reform strategies.

10. Susan J. Bodilly and others, *Lessons from New American Schools' Scale-Up Phase: Prospects for Bringing Designs to Multiple Schools* (Santa Monica, Calif.: RAND, 1998).

11. Milton Friedman and Rose Friedman, *Free to Choose* (Harcourt Brace Jovanovich, 1980).

12. Chester E. Finn, Bruno V. Manno, and Gregg Vanourek, *Charter Schools in Action: Renewing Public Education* (Princeton University Press, 2000).

Chapter Two

1. The descriptions included in this chapter are very brief. Longer versions of each case study can be found in the appendix. At present, conditions in each district are changing, some dramatically. For the purposes of this volume, however, the descriptions represent a snapshot of the district issues, successes, and challenges each faced early in 1999.

2. For more detail, see John H. Stanford and Robin Simons, *Victory in Our Schools: We Can Give Our Children Excellent Public Eduction* (Bantam Books, 1999).

3. For reports on the three earlier studies see Paul T. Hill, Leslie Shapiro, and Arthur E. Wise, *Educational Progress: Cities Mobilize to Improve Their Schools* (Santa Monica, Calif.: RAND, 1989); Paul T. Hill and Josephine J. Bonan, *Decentralization and Accountability in Public Education* (Santa Monica, Calif.: RAND, 1991); and Anthony S. Bryk and others, *Improving School-Community Connections: Moving toward a System of Community Schools* (Baltimore: Annie E. Casey Foundation, 1999).

Chapter Three

1. See, for example, Lorraine M. McDonnell and Anthony Pascal, *Teacher Unions and Educational Reform* (Santa Monica, Calif.: RAND, 1988).

2. For a more detailed analysis of the simulations see Sara H. Taggart, "School Reform in Edgeport: An Education Reform Strategy-Building Session. Findings and Discussion" (Seattle: Center on Reinventing Public Education, 1998). The discussion here borrows liberally from Taggart's paper.

Chapter Four

1. This study focuses on strategies for school improvement. It does not directly address other factors (poverty, for example, or language background) that might affect students' learning. A suc-

cessful strategy addressing all these problems could have more dramatic effects on student learning than a school improvement strategy alone.

2. Anthony S. Bryk and others, *Improving School-Community Connections: Moving toward a System of Community Schools* (Baltimore: Annie E. Casey Foundation, 1999). See also Betty Malen and Rodney T. Ogawa, "Professional-Patron Influence on Site-Based Governance Councils: A Confounding Case Study," *Educational Evaluation and Policy Analysis*, vol. 10 (Winter 1989), pp. 251–70; and Paul T. Hill and Josephine J. Bonan, *Decentralization and Accountability in Public Education* (Santa Monica, Calif.: RAND, 1991).

3. See Paul T. Hill and Mary Beth Celio, *Fixing Urban Schools* (Brookings, 1998), chap. 4, for a discussion of the weakness of evidence against such popular options as choice and competition.

4. The Education Commission of the States (a Denver-based interstate compact) has convened a National Commission on School Governance Reform that is developing options similar to those presented here. The commission's report, issued in November 1999, provides detailed analyses of options and suggestions for implementation. Local leaders using this book as a guide to strategy formation should also obtain the ECS Commission report and supporting materials. See National Commission on Governing America's Schools, *Governing America's Schools:Changing the Rules* (Denver: Education Commission of the States, 1999).

5. For detailed analyses of Chicago and Charlotte see Bryk and others, *Improving School-Community Connections*.

6. In District 2 some schools were able to perform these functions, not because they had the formal power to do so but because Alvarado knew how to help them beat the system.

7. See, for example, Paul T. Hill, Lawrence C. Pierce, and James W. Guthrie, *Reinventing Public Education: How Contracting Can Transform America's Schools* (University of Chicago Press, 1997); John Brandl, *Money and Good Intentions Are Not Enough* (Brookings, 1998); and Chester E. Finn, Bruno V. Manno, and Gregg Vanourek, *Charter Schools in Action: Renewing Public Education* (Princeton University Press, 2000).

8. For a more complete analysis of this option see Lawrence C. Pierce, "A Community Education Board," prepared for the Education Commission of the States' National Commission on Governing America's Schools, July 1999.

9. John E. Chubb and Terry M. Moe were the first of many to address this question. See their *Politics, Markets, and America's Schools* (Brookings, 1990). See also Hill, Pierce, and Guthrie, *Reinventing Public Education*.

10. Frederick M. Hess, *Spinning Wheels: The Politics of Urban School Reform* (Brookings, 1999), pp. 178–81.

11. Paul T. Hill, "Supplying Effective Public Schools in Big Cities," in Diane Ravitch, ed., *Brookings Papers on Education Policy, 1999* (Brookings, 1999), p. 422.

Chapter Five

1. See Anthony S. Bryk and others, *Charting Chicago School Reform: Democratic Localism as a Lever for Change* (Boulder, Colo.: Westview Press, 1998).

2. See Anthony S. Bryk and others, *Improving School-Community Connections: Moving toward a System of Community Schools* (Baltimore: Annie E. Casey Foundation, 1999); Paul T. Hill and Paula Wolf, *Support Structures in a Reformed School System* (Chicago Finance Authority, 1991); Donald R. McAdams, "Lessons from Houston," in Diane Ravitch, ed., *Brookings Papers on Education Policy, 1999* (Brookings, 1999); David T. Kearns and James Harvey, *A Legacy of Learning: Your Stake in Standards and New Kinds of Public Schools* (Brookings, 1999); and Chester E. Finn, Bruno V. Manno, and Gregg Vanourek, *Charter Schools in Action: Renewing Public Education* (Princeton University Press, 2000).

3. Bryk and others, *Charting Chicago School Reform*, p. 283, provides a good summary of the CEO–Strong Schools superintendent's role: "Supporting improvements in the operation of exist-

ing schools, promoting promising start-ups in the form of new and alternative schools, and eliminating its weakest units (i.e., ineffective schools)."

4. Bryk and others, *Charting Chicago School Reform*, p. 298.

5. Bryk and others, *Charting Chicago School Reform*, p. 283: "A system of schools conjures up images of educational federalism where individual schools, operating as recognized legal entities, have a direct voice in crafting the rules by which the whole system runs."

6. For a detailed discussion of the accountability challenges faced by schools operating in a marketlike environment see Paul T. Hill, Lawrence C. Pierce, and Robin J. Lake, *How Are Public Charter Schools Held Accountable?* (University of Washington Center on Reinventing Public Education, 1998).

7. For a full analysis of school-teacher relations under models 2 or 3 see Paul T. Hill, Lawrence C. Pierce, and James W. Guthrie, *Reinventing Public Education: How Contracting Can Transform America's Schools* (University of Chicago Press, 1997).

8. See Paul T. Hill and Robin J. Lake, *Toward a K–12 Educational Accountability System for Washington State* (Seattle: Center on Reinventing Public Education, 1997).

9. On human development see Wise and Darling-Hammond performance assessment and analysis of options studies. Arthur E. Wise and Linda Darling-Hammond, "Teacher Evaluation and Teacher Professionalism," *Educational Leadership*, vol. 42, no. 4 (1985), pp. 28–33.

10. Bryk and others, *Charting Chicago School Reform*.

11. See Charles Taylor Kerchner, Julia E. Koppich, and Joseph G. Weeres, *United Mind Workers: Unions and Teaching in the Knowledge Society* (San Francisco : Jossey-Bass, 1997).

Chapter Six

1. For an extended discussion of these issues see Paul T. Hill, *How to Create Incentives for Design-Based Schools* (Arlington, Va.: New American Schools, 1997).

2. This explains Frederick Hess's finding that school system insiders rate all kinds of reforms, including those that have not succeeded in improving schools, as more fully carried out than do other observers like newspaper education reporters. See *Spinning Wheels: The Politics of Urban School Reform* (Brookings, 1998), p. 171.

3. Brookings will publish a book in late 2000 providing detailed guidance for the organization and work of the independent analysis agency.

4. Authors' calculations based on Mary Beth Celio, *Random Acts of Kindness? External Resources Available to the Seattle Public Schools* (University of Washington Center on Reinventing Public Education, 1996), p. 5.

5. For a more detailed list of necessary changes in state law and policy see Paul T. Hill, Lawrence C. Pierce, and James W. Guthrie, *Reinventing Public Education: How Contracting Can Transform America's Schools* (University of Chicago Press, 1997), chap. 7.

6. All these things happened in the course of one small reform initiative in Seattle. A philanthropist who offered to pay millions of dollars for total redevelopment of a failing low-income school was forced by a grassroots scare campaign to withdraw his offer and try again later. He tried and succeeded the next year only by appealing directly to parents and grandparents, not relying on district administrators to carry the message about what was offered and what it would mean for the school's current students.

Chapter Seven

1. See the final chapter of Paul T. Hill and Mary Beth Celio, *Fixing Urban Schools* (Brookings, 1998), for suggestions about how private sector leaders can make sure that they apply the same rigor in the actions toward school reform as they do toward proposals in their own businesses.

2. Frederick M. Hess, *Spinning Wheels: The Politics of Urban School Reform* (Brookings, 1999).

3. For the ECS program call Thomas Jandris (303) 299-3600.

4. For the CPRE program call Richard Elmore (617) 496-4814.

5. For the Brookings program, call Paul Hill (206) 685-2214.

Appendix

1. H. D. S. Greenway, "Boston's New Superintendent," *Boston Globe,* August 5, 1995, p. 8.

2. See (www.boston.k12.ma.us/supt/payzant.asp [November 11, 1999]). During his decade-long tenure in San Diego, a district twice the size of Boston, he was praised by parents and educators for having "fostered or championed a steady stream of new ideas and innovative programs." Under Payzant, central office staff shrank by 31 percent and the power structure was shifted so that schools had more decisionmaking power. Some of his opponents in San Diego suggested that his primary goal of closing the gap between minority and white students' test scores was "a dismal failure," but his San Diego legacy was generally good. The former San Diego School Board president went so far as to suggest that Payzant "walks on water." Adam Pertman, "San Diego Leaders Give Payzant an 'A' for Effort," *Boston Globe,* August 10, 1995, p. 1.

3. In May 1998 five of the seventeen high schools were on probation relative to their accreditation from the New England Association of Schools and Colleges, and one school, the Jeremiah E. Burke High School, lost its accreditation in 1995.

4. All demographic data are from Boston Public Schools (BPS) analysis of students by race and grade, May 13, 1998.

5. Metropolitan Achievement and Stanford 9 test scores cannot be psychometrically compared. Thus the baseline for the impact of these reform efforts began with the introduction of the Stanford 9 in 1995.

6. Payzant has set a goal that the average test scores of all racial achievement groups be within 5 percentage points by the 2003 school year.

7. "The Quest for Excellence in Boston Public Schools: A Guideline for Results," *Boston Globe,* August 2, 1995.

8. The Annenberg Foundation specified that its $10 million support three reform efforts already in place in Boston: pilot schools, 21st Century Schools (the first cohort of twenty-seven schools sponsored by the Boston Plan for Excellence), and the Center for Leadership Development (a joint labor-management professional development center). (www.boston.k12.ma.us/bps/whole_change. asp [December 1, 1999]).

9. *FOCUS* (a newsletter for Boston's Annenberg Challenge Schools), Spring 1998.

10. *Boston Public Schools Plan for Whole-School Change,* Working document 2-99, developed by Boston Public Schools and the Annenberg Foundation (www.bpe.org/pubs/misc/wscchart.pdf [December 1, 1999]).

11. The distinction between clusters and cohorts can be confusing. Clusters were created in 1997 and represent groups of schools (ten in each) that divide the schools into geographic regions. Like breaking high schools into schools within schools, the purpose of clusters was to increase collegiality and communication among schools. Cohorts represent groups of schools at various stages of reform. The first cohort of twenty-seven schools was deemed the most ready to begin school change in 1996. Three cohorts followed, twenty-five schools each in three successive years, until all the schools were involved in the whole-school change.

12. Fleet Bank is working in partnership with the Harvard Graduate School of Education to provide leadership training for teachers in BPS. They are currently working in twenty schools.

13. Boston Municipal Research Bureau, "Raising the Bar for Education in Boston," no. 98-3, April 8, 1998.

14. Of ninth graders who began school in 1993, 26.4 percent did not graduate in 1997. Office of Research, Assessment, and Evaluation, "Q and A: Student Dropout in the Boston Public Schools: 1997–98" (Boston Public Schools: March 1999).

15. BPS will conduct in-depth reviews each year of 25 percent of schools "not meeting standards" and a review of all schools within four years.

16. A second-year evaluation indicates that the first year's results have continued. The second cohort of schools implementing whole-school designs demonstrated substantial improvement, and the schools in their second year of implementation (the first cohort) demonstrated the most improvement.

17. For more detail, see Donna Harrington-Lueker, "Keeping House in Memphis," *Executive Educator*, October 1994, pp. 32–34.

18. Although NAS designs were intended to cost no more than current school expenditures, initial implementation has proven costly, involving significant expenditures for staff training and consultation services for school designers.

19. See the mission statement at (www.memphis-schools.k12.tn.us [December 6, 1999]).

20. The district has established goals and objectives for student achievement levels in reading and language arts, mathematics, science, and social studies, and for increases in promotion and attendance rates and decreases in dropout rates.

21. Lynn Olson, "Memphis Study Tracks Gains in Whole School Designs," *Education Week on the Web*, May 27, 1998 (www.edweek.org).

22. Interview with Gerry House, June 12, 1998.

23. As quoted in Richard F. Elmore and Deanna Burney, "School Variation and Systemic Instructional Improvement in Community School District #2, New York City," University of Pittsburgh, Learning Research and Development Center, 1997, p. 5.

24. Laura Williams, "Ex-Schools Chief California-Bound," *Daily News*, June 16, 1998, p. 28.

25. Demographic data summarized from Elmore and Burney, "School Variation," p. 12.

26. Elmore and Burney, "School Variation," p. 13.

27. Mary Kay Stein, "High-Performance Learning Communities, District 2: Report on Year One Implementation of School Learning Communities," University of Pittsburgh, Learning Research and Development Center, 1998.

28. Stein, "High-Performance Learning Communities," p. 3, paraphrase of comment made by district leaders.

29. Elmore and Burney, "School Variation," p. 8. District 2 video reports that some schools are visited up to six times a year if necessary.

30. This is a principle that was made clear in interview with Alvarado and is echoed in the literature. See Elmore and Burney, "School Variation," and Stein, "High-Performance Learning Communities."

31. Stein, "High-Performance Learning Communities."

32. As cited in Stein, "High-Performance Learning Communities," p. 7.

33. Elmore and Burney, "School Variation," p. 20.

34. Stein, "High-Performance Learning Communities," p. 4.

35. Stein, "High-Performance Learning Communities," p. 5.

36. U.S. Education Secretary Richard Riley announced that Texas received a $12 million federal grant to encourage the kind of reforms Superintendent Diana Lam has pushed in the San Antonio School District. Jeanne Russell, "Lam Innovations at SASD Praised," *San Antonio Express News*, September 3, 1998, p. 8.

37. San Antonio has been awarded funding for major initiatives by the Rockefeller Foundation, National Commission on Teaching and America's Future, Spencer Foundation, and National Science Foundation. The district has forged partnerships with Trinity University and University of Texas, San Antonio. It is being studied by the RAND Corporation and the University of Washington.

38. San Francisco Unified School District Recommended Budget, June 1998.

39. Ann Bradley, "Learning on the Job," *Education Week*, February 15, 1995.

40. Caroline Hendrie, "A Mixed Record for Reconstitution Flashes a Yellow Light for Districts," *Education Week*, July 8, 1998.

41. Dick Lilly, "School's Ending, but District Still Has Plenty to Do," *Seattle Times*, June 18, 1998.

42. Dick Lilly, "Seattle Ending School Busing," *Seattle Times*, November 21, 1996.

Index